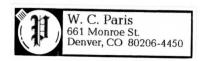
BUILDING ON SOLID GROUND

D0980905

Building on
SOLID
GROUND

Authentic Values and
How to Attain Them

THOMAS D. WILLIAMS, LC

ALBA · HOUSE   NEW · YORK

SOCIETY OF ST. PAUL, 2187 VICTORY BLVD., STATEN ISLAND, NEW YORK 10314

Library of Congress Cataloging-in-Publication Data

Williams, Thomas D., LC
    Building on solid ground: authentic values and how to attain
    them / Thomas D. Williams.
        p.   cm.
    ISBN 0-8189-0749-5
    1. Values.   2. Ethics.   3. Christian ethics — Catholic authors.
    I. Title.
    BJ1031.W525   1995
    241 — dc20   95-33111
                                                          CIP

Produced and designed in the United States of America by the
Fathers and Brothers of the Society of St. Paul,
2187 Victory Boulevard, Staten Island, New York 10314,
as part of their communications apostolate.

ISBN: 0-8189-0749-5

Printing Information:

Current Printing - first digit   1   2   3   4   5   6   7   8   9   10

Year of Current Printing - first year shown

1995   1996   1997   1998   1999   2000

"It is urgently necessary, for the future of society and the development of a sound democracy, to rediscover those essential and innate human and moral values which flow from the very truth of the human being and express and safeguard the dignity of the person: values which no individual, no majority and no State can ever create, modify or destroy, but must only acknowledge, respect and promote."

— POPE JOHN PAUL II
Encyclical letter
Evangelium Vitae 71

CONTENTS

Introduction ix

Chapter 1: The Value of Values 1
    Price and Value 2
    The Real Thing 7
    The Modern Crisis 9
    Human Values 20
    A Hierarchy of Values 23
    A Christian Perspective 28

Chapter 2: The Foundation of Value 33
    Nature 34
    Finality or Purpose 36
    The Foundation of Value 37
    Who is Man? 39
    The Meaning of Life 43
    Keeping Shipshape 46

Chapter 3: Freedom and Values 55
    The Many Faces of Freedom 57
    Three Levels of Freedom 59
    The Value of Liberty 64
    Odd Bedfellows? 67
    The Truth Will Set You Free 73

Freedom and Christianity 75
The Greatest Triumph 77
Cultivating Personal Freedom 78

Chapter 4: VALUES IN ACTION:
           MAKING CHOICES 81

What's in a Choice? 82
The Big Four 91
Fundamental Option 99
Solid Decisions 101

Chapter 5: MORAL VALUE 107

Right and Wrong 108
The Real You 112
Moral Eyesight 115
The Role of Conscience 121
Fine Tuning 122
Moral Obligation 125
A Matter of Perspective 127
Legalism vs. Love 129

Chapter 6: HARMONY OF THE
           HUMAN PERSON 133

Maturity Myths 135
In Search of a Definition 137
A Light Generation 142
When I Was a Child. 146
The Pattern to Follow 163

Chapter 7: IN PURSUIT OF HAPPINESS 165

Is Everybody Happy? 166
Degrees of Happiness 169
Treasure Hunting 176
Three Fruitful Fields 183

INTRODUCTION

In 1972 Sydney Simon published a seemingly innocuous book entitled *Values Clarification: A Handbook of Practical Strategies for Teachers and Students*. Thus began a tragic social experiment whose effects are still being felt today.

There were two simple premises behind this experiment. The first was that if children were left to their own natural inclinations, their innate attraction to goodness would allow a fully developed, mature value system to spontaneously emerge. The second was that values are wholly personal, and thus the teacher's values shouldn't be imposed on children, but the children should be allowed to formulate their own values. The outcome has been one of the highest rates of juvenile crime, delinquency, drug abuse, gratuitous violence and sexual promiscuity that the world has ever seen.

Almost everyone agrees that a well-formed value system is a fundamental requirement for a happy, fulfilling, directed life. There is also agreement that values play a critical role in our decision-making. As Aristotle concluded more than two millennia ago, the reasonable man (that is, the vast majority of us) acts for a purpose. When we act, we pursue something that seems good to us. This is true for everyday actions as well as for our most transcendent decisions such as the choice of a spouse.

One person's goal in life could be to amass the largest quantity of possessions possible. This would be the key value that directs his decisions. Another may seek to maximize personal pleasure and minimize pain. Still another may spend his days and energy on the advance of science or art or music. A person's values, whichever they are, play a key role in his choices and the character he forges for himself.

While there is a basic consensus as to the importance of the role of values, the disagreement begins as soon as we start talking about *what* values are and *how* to achieve a balanced scale of values. The underlying assumptions of Simon's book — that values are solely a matter of individual discernment, that they depend on the vagaries of time and circumstance, and that each person creates his own values — represent a prevalent misconception. Reason and experience indicate otherwise. And in actual fact, our modern culture is itself premised on a well-ordered but seldom-questioned materialistic value system.

Because of current sensibilities, many are afraid to qualify any particular value scale as better than another, and prefer to leave values up to individual tastes. This is the relativistic, values-clarification approach. The obvious problem is that this method can never lead to the desired outcome: a coherent, well-formed value system. Then again, if values are simply a matter of personal preference, there is no sense in bemoaning delinquency, drug abuse and violence, since these "values" are presumably no worse than any others.

In the present political and cultural climate where a sort of institutional relativism reigns, we are told that not only beauty, but also truth, goodness, right and wrong are in the eyes of the beholder. This mentality has been pawned off on our children and the results have been catastrophic. The strange thing is, that while this absolute relativism sounds very nice in theory, in practice no one lives it in his or her own life. Paradoxically, the staunchest relativists are often given to the most dogmatic affirmations.

This book follows a different premise: that some values are really and truly preferable to others, that some pursuits elevate and others degrade us. For this reason, it is more profitable to search for the truth, even when it is hard to find, than to give in to the temptation of a superficial utilitarianism that ignores life's more important questions.

This is not an academic work. It is meant to be a practical guide to help better understand what values are, to offer criteria to discern between different options and to suggest ways to organize our lives around values that are worthy of our dignity as human persons.

In our search for authenticity, some fundamental questions arise. The key to happiness lies in finding the answers to these questions, as well as in recognizing their practical consequences and acting upon them.

- Are there real values or does everything just depend on one's point of view?
- Who or what is man and how does human nature affect values?
- Is freedom just open license to do as I please or is there more to it?
- How can I make solid choices in my life in accord with my values and principles?
- How can I integrate my values, decisions and actions into a balanced, mature personality?
- In what does happiness consist and how can I go about reaching it?

In examining these encompassing topics, I will draw upon our common human experience as well as upon some of history's great writers and observers of the human condition. In particular, I will look to our Christian heritage and the example and teachings of Jesus Christ. This does not mean that this text is directed only to Christians, but rather it offers to all persons of good will the opportunity to examine the challenges of the human condition under the illumination of the Christian perspective.

BUILDING ON SOLID GROUND

CHAPTER 1

THE VALUE OF VALUES

A great deal of attention has been given to the topic of values in recent years, particularly in the public forum, and rightly so. The very word and its kindred (such as *valuable*) suggest something of tremendous importance and interest. Public figures routinely pepper emotion-packed speeches with references to "family values," "the values upon which this country was founded," "the core values of our society" and the like. We are instinctively attracted by these expressions because they seem to convey something very fundamental, something that lies at the root of our human experience.

But however appealing the word may be, it is difficult to nail down exactly what we mean by "values." While this ambiguity may be convenient for politicians who use the term for its emotional impact, for the rest of us it can be terribly unsettling to have such a vital concept remain so vague.

1

One of the reasons for our uncertainty about values is that the term has moved back and forth freely between two realms — between the economic realm and the realm of human experience. Although a cursory review seems to indicate that the concept is the same in both cases, a more careful analysis reveals that there are substantial differences, which are critical to a proper understanding of values in the human sphere.

PRICE AND VALUE

In economic terms, value is a simple concept to grasp. It is closely allied to "price," and we are fortunate to have a medium of exchange (money) that allows us to place any property or service on a universal scale of value. The relative price of any two items allows us to determine which is more "valuable," and how disparate the values are.

In our ordinary experience, the market proves to be fairly efficient and closely ties the price of merchandise to the underlying costs of raw materials, design, manufacturing and distribution. This suggests that an item's value is something intrinsic to the item, something that does not depend on our individual estimation, but rather on objective, measurable facts. And in general, our behavior as consumers reflects this assumption.

You might spend $150,000 for a Ferrari, but

you wouldn't think of spending so much for a Honda. And the reason you would give is, because "it's not worth it." If you were at a store and found 26-inch color televisions selling for $50 each, you might be tempted to buy out the entire inventory. If asked why you bought so many televisions when you only needed one, you might say, "They're worth at least ten times that much." And you would probably (rightly) assume that you could resell the extra nine to other eager buyers for much more than $50, since they would readily recognize the underlying *value* of the televisions.

However, as soon as we begin exploring beyond the realm of commodities, the picture is no longer so clear. What determines the value of a masterpiece by Van Gogh? The cost of the canvas and pigments can be no more than a few dollars. No matter how lofty a wage we assign to the artist's labor, we cannot even approach the price such a painting might command at auction. Other paintings upon which lesser artists labored many times longer do not attract bidders at even a small fraction of the price.

We have now crossed over into an area where price (and value) are a matter of someone's judgment. Individual artists may go in and out of favor, and the prices of their works correspondingly rise and fall, with no change whatsoever in the actual paintings.

Since prices are ruled by the law of supply

and demand, the value of goods is often actually determined by how highly they are esteemed, or by how popular they are — thus, values become almost completely *subjective*. That is, they depend not so much on the product itself as on the buyer's desire for the product.

When consumers in the early 1980s lost interest in buying prerecorded music on eight-track tapes, the street price plummeted and they were quickly relegated to 25-cent bargain bins. It didn't matter that they cost several dollars to manufacture, or even that the artist received a royalty of a dollar or more for each one.

In the late '50s and '60s hula-hoops were the rage (for those who don't remember, a hula-hoop is a plastic ring which rotates around the waist and is kept up by vigorously gyrating the midriff). Retailers were able to sell tens of thousands for several dollars each. Except for this peculiar fad, these hoops were practically worthless and served no other function.

Another objectively worthless item, the "Pet Rock," was introduced in the '70s and was simply a clever marketing scheme to sell otherwise worthless chunks of granite, giving them appeal by providing them with names, instructions and an appropriate habitat. Countless other examples of this phenomenon could be cited, from yo-yos to moon boots to "Cabbage Patch" dolls.

Prices depend on consumers' perceptions

and tastes, because economic value, like beauty, is in the eyes of the beholder. At a dog fair held in Milan, Italy in March, 1993, a German shepherd named Fanto was awarded the "Golden Collar." He is thought by many to be the most beautiful example of German shepherd-dom of all time. His price: one billion two hundred thousand lira, or something over $750,000.

One may inquire what the difference is between Fanto the wonder pup and Kranz the German shepherd down the street that only costs $150. They're both about the same size and color, eat the same food, and will both die and be buried within the next ten years or so. Substantially there really is no difference, but to certain dog connoisseurs Fanto is in a league by himself.

And this isn't a matter only of gimmicks or luxury items; demand, and hence price, fluctuates in every consumer sector from the housing market to the trading of precious metals. It's enough to remember the staggering fluctuations in gold prices in the early '80s to realize that even for durable goods there is no guaranteed stability. Consumers' desires and perceptions are volatile and go up and down like the mercury in a thermometer.

All this is fine for an economic system, but can it legitimately be transferred to the realm of human values? Life offers countless values to which we cannot attach a price tag. How much would one pay for a strong, united family? How much is a faithful husband worth? As the Beatles' song goes, "Money can't buy me love." Are these values — human values, religious values, moral values and the like — based on the same subjective principle of personal desire?

Many would say yes. In fact, the economic model is the prevailing conception of values in modern society. Values are often considered to be a wholly personal affair, a creation of individual or collective desires and preferences. In this way values have been reduced to a mere expression of personal sentiment, like the subjective preference a person may have for one color over another, or one sport over another.

Others consider values to have an element of stability and objectivity. This allows them to be qualified as good or bad, deep or shallow, superior or inferior.

In essence it comes down to the question of whether some things in life *really* are better than others, or whether some things are worth pursuing and others not. If in reality everything is arbitrary, if there is no inherent difference in value between honesty and dishonesty, war and peace, education and ignorance, then it is senseless to speak of values in an objective way.

We could highlight two problems with the application of the economic-value model to human values in general. The first is its radical subjectivity which divorces values from the reality of human existence. In the case of commodities, values fluctuate. When we're dealing with human values, bound up closely to our human nature, there is necessarily more continuity. Though jogging or diet fads may go in and out of style, health will always be a value to the human person.

A second difficulty stems from the attempt to place all values on an equal footing, as if they were commensurate. This process works in economics because all consumer products are transferred to a common scale through the use of a medium of exchange. In the case of human values, however, this mechanism is impracticable. The value of sincerity simply cannot be weighed against, for instance, a good lunch. Sincerity and food are both values but they are on essentially different levels.

THE REAL THING

Genuine values are not only based on the subjective factor of desire, but also on the objective element of intrinsic worth. As a working definition we could say that a value is *a good recognized and appreciated as a good*, or simply, *a good for me*.

Two dimensions can readily be distinguished: (1) a value must *be* something good (objective dimension), and (2) I must *recognize* its goodness for me (subjective dimension). Both dimensions are essential.

Something good that I don't recognize or appreciate as good for me, will not attract me or move me to action. Therefore it is not a value for me. Niccolò Machiavelli, the Renaissance political theorist and author of *The Prince*, didn't appreciate honesty because he saw it as an obstacle to efficient government. Thus, honesty — something good in itself — didn't constitute a value for his life because he failed to recognize its goodness.

On the other hand, a true value must be objectively good. One may be attracted by something that appears good but in reality is not. Though some drug addicts may desire heroin passionately, it can never be a true value because it harms them as persons.

Therefore values are not purely objective, independent of the human person, nor are they purely subjective, the creation of one's desires. Both factors are necessary.

This principle is illustrated in some of the Gospel parables, for example the parable of the treasure in the field: "The Kingdom of God is like a treasure buried in a field which someone has found; he hides it again, goes off happy, sells everything he owns and buys that field" (Mt 13:44).

This brings out the two facets of values. First we see that a value (in this case the Kingdom of

God, the supreme value) is above all a find, a discovery. What is unearthed is a treasure, a real treasure. The treasure is not a creation of human endeavor, nor a product of human fantasy or desire. It is desired precisely because it is desirable.

Secondly, we have the finder, the man who recognizes the treasure. What sort of person is he? He must be able to identify a treasure when he sees one and distinguish between true riches and rubbish. Ravens are attracted by bright, shiny objects and hoard them in their nests, but it makes no difference to a raven if what shines is the foil from a chewing gum wrapper or an 18-carat gold chain. A raven has no appreciation for objective value. Often we fall into the same delusion. Like the ravens we chase after appearances of worth that attract the senses but do not satisfy the heart. As Shakespeare reminds us, "All that glitters is not gold." Not all that seems to be good is good indeed.

THE MODERN CRISIS

The idea that values are a creation of the individual can be traced to the theories of several existentialist philosophers (Nietzsche, Heidegger, Sartre, de Beauvoir, Polin). It is also present in psychological schools of thought, notably in Carl Rogers and Abraham Maslow. In the '60s, '70s and

'80s this ideological current pervaded the educational system and became the prevailing popular model.

In schools, instead of learning to recognize *real* values and put them into practice in their own lives, students have been encouraged to clarify their *personal* values, with no necessary reference to objective reality. Teachers, in turn, have been prompted to foster open thinking in young people by adopting a non-directive, non-judgmental approach to values.

This technique has been applied to sexual ethics, respect for parents and authorities, drug use, abortion, euthanasia and numerous other aspects of human life. The effects have been so broad and sweeping that many simply have no concept of good and bad, right and wrong. As the French author André Frossard said, "The first premise of modernity is that there are no values, no values at all, only options and opinions." That is to say, we have lost a sense of objective values, and only see those that each person creates for himself.

Can you imagine a chemistry class in which the teacher blithely announces to the students, "Salt is designated NaCl because it is generally believed to be composed of sodium and chlorine. Of course if you don't agree, you're free to submit any other combination of elements and we will hold your opinion in equal regard to that of the majority"?

This scenario is, of course, unthinkable. Underlying contemporary educational practice is the firm conviction that mathematics, natural sciences and all empirically verifiable data pertain to the realm of "knowledge" — which can be taught with relative certainty — while religion, ethics, metaphysics and the like are strictly matters of opinion and personal inclination. For such a mentality, values are determined not by any objective reality but by what each individual accepts or chooses to believe. This is tantamount to asserting that there simply is no absolute good for man.

Despite modern society's claim to total impartiality as regards values, there are, nonetheless, at least two values which are frequently presented to us as absolute: the value of *tolerance* and the value of *pluralism*.

Tolerance or a Cheap Substitute?

Tolerance for others and for their ideas is often promoted as the supreme and unequivocal good. Tolerance is indeed very good, though it isn't the *only* good. The tragedy is that what often passes for tolerance really isn't tolerance at all. What many deem tolerance is nothing more than *indifference* or *skepticism*.

Indifference is simply not caring, not being interested in others. "Anyone can believe whatever he wants as long as he doesn't hurt anyone else." (Especially not *me*.) This attitude is reflected, for example, in Voltaire's writings on tolerance. Voltaire equated tolerance with, in today's language, minding one's own business. He took St. Thomas Aquinas to task as being intolerant for having dared to say that he wished all the world were Christian. But for St. Thomas that is the same as saying he wished all men to be happy. I suppose no one would consider it intolerant to wish all men to be healthy or well-educated (though this implies intolerance towards ignorance and illness). True tolerance in no way implies indifference to the lot of our brothers and sisters.

Skepticism, on the other hand, is doubt regarding the existence of truth, or at least as to our ability to ascertain it. Personal values are relegated to the realm of "opinion," as opposed to "fact." Facts can be taught; opinions are a personal matter and are best kept to oneself.

This mentality can be traced in part back to John Locke, an influential British philosopher of the 17th century. In his classic letter on religious tolerance Locke propounded tolerance as necessary for the peaceful functioning of society. His grounds for tolerance, however, were the conviction that we simply *cannot know* who is right or wrong — hence one theory is as admissible as any other. This is skepticism and not tolerance.

Much of the confusion stems from the failure to distinguish between respect for some*one* and respect for someone's *ideas*. They are not the same thing. Ideas must *earn* respect, persons *deserve* it because of their dignity as children of God. You don't need to prove your worth to me or earn my love. The very fact that you are a human person, created by God out of love in his image and likeness — that is enough for me.

But ideas? They come in all shapes and sizes: true and false, ridiculous and compelling, brilliant and commonplace, diabolical and divine. I respect you and defend your right to follow your conscience because God has made you free and worthy of respect. But I unhesitatingly evaluate your ideas on their own merit. Some are acceptable, others should be rejected as untenable.

Authentic tolerance doesn't demand that we abandon our convictions but rather that we respect the inviolability of others' consciences and their right to follow their beliefs. It also implies the acknowledgment of the intrinsic evil in using force to make others change their mind, even when we *know* they are mistaken.

It is incorrect to say that plausible theories are tolerated; they are rather accepted as reasonable in their own right. Errors, on the other hand, *are* sometimes tolerated — in deference to a greater good: for example, respect for the human person.

This is the essence of genuine tolerance. With consideration for others we should make an effort to lead them to a more fulfilling existence through the pursuit of higher values.

A final problem with touting tolerance as an absolute value is simply that not everything should be tolerated. We don't tolerate smallpox or child abuse or oil spills, or thousands of other social evils. George Bernard Shaw writes, "We may prate of toleration as we will; but society must always draw a line somewhere between allowable conduct and insanity or crime."

Plurality or Pluralism?

Along with tolerance, another value promulgated by contemporary society is *pluralism*. Pluralism can be understood in two ways. One is the objective recognition that diversity exists. The second sees an ever greater diversity as an ideal to be pursued.

According to the first meaning, pluralism is simply acknowledgment that *plurality* exists and different ways of thinking and behaving should be taken into account. Different people have different needs and we ought to be considerate of the particular necessities of all, and not just of those who are like us.

The other type of pluralism takes the form of an ideology. This ideology maintains that a perfect or ideal society is necessarily made up of the widest range of values possible. Variety is good. Uniformity is bad.

At first glance this seems to be true and proponents' arguments are convincing. After all, is not variety the spice of life? They would say that a diversity of values adds to the beauty of society the way a diversity of flowers adds to the beauty of a flower garden or the way a variety of instruments enhances the beauty of an orchestra. Vivaldi's *Four Seasons* certainly wouldn't have the same vitality and charm if it were played by a solo alto bassoon. A variety of interests and hobbies also embellishes culture.

We run into two difficulties, however, if we try to apply this principle across the board to values. First of all, is variety an absolute good? It would seem that it is good only insofar as it completes and perfects the whole. In the example of the flower garden, it is true that the addition of different strains of flowers adds to the overall beauty and harmony of the whole — but only because each is beautiful *in itself*.

What would happen if we were to strew beer cans, plastic bags and orange rinds among the flowers? Variety would increase but overall beauty would plummet. The same would occur if in the case of our orchestra we were to introduce a police whistle or a jackhammer. These measures would certainly boost the variety but would spoil the harmony of the whole. That is why musical pieces are "variations on a theme." An order is necessary and the individual parts must themselves be of value.

Likewise a human value is what completes and perfects human nature and contributes to the harmony of the person. Variety is only good when the individual elements that compose it are good.

No organism can be built upon diversity alone. Unity is strength, division weakens. The founding fathers of America selected as motto for the incipient nation the phrase *E pluribus unum*, literally rendered in English "From many, one." This choice clearly manifests the diversity of origin and culture of the populace.

At the same time we can't help but notice the clearly uni-directional process represented by the expression, which is a process not of *homogenization* but of *unification*. Many individuals, from many different sociological and cultural backgrounds, come together to form a nation based on certain common values. Here there is no trace of our modern multi-culturalism that seeks to underscore differences. Rather we see the desire to form a union, enriched by the natural diversity of its members.

The strength of any association, nation or society can be measured by its fundamental unity of purpose and ideals. "Divide and conquer," the Roman slogan that summed up an effective military strategy, gives us a clue to the eventual effects of deliberately seeking internal division. As experience shows — Bosnia and Rwanda come to mind —little fruit can be drawn from the accentuation of differences besides conflict, hatred and war.

The second fallacy of this rationale is the assumption that uniformity is always bad. I would argue that *conformism* and *nonconformism* are poor standards for action, whereas uniformity can be good or bad depending on other factors.

Conformists and nonconformists are not opposites, although they might appear to be. They merely sing two versions of the same song. Their main flaw is that they take others' behavior as the criterion for their actions, rather than appealing to their own principles. The conformist sees what others are doing and does the same. The nonconformist sees what others are doing and automatically does something else. But both of these modes of behavior are manifestations of insecurity and over-dependence on others. The conformist and his counterpart relinquish their personal freedom to fashion, to public opinion, to what is socially acceptable, instead of making decisions based on their own convictions.

Uniformity, on the other hand, is natural and good if what everyone is choosing is a value in itself. If no one cheats on Mrs. Twizzler's French test and Johnny doesn't cheat either, that doesn't mean he's a crowd follower or a victim of peer pressure. He is honest because honesty is a value in itself. His decision is independent of what the others are doing.

If everyone in society were loyal and fair and hard-working we would have more uniformity, but society wouldn't for that reason become dull or insipid. Uniformity or "sameness" is secondary. I do what I believe to be good independently of what the others do. If they are doing the same thing — fine. If not, why should that alter my behavior?

Freedom or Anarchy?

There is a deeper and more far-reaching problem with a purely subjective concept of values. If we affirm that there is no good for man outside of his personal, individual desires, we are setting the stage for anarchy. Society may propose tolerance as a principle, but there will always be those who do not see things in the same light. And since values cannot be "imposed," the intolerant person has as much right to his standards as the tolerant. The same can be said for the anti-Semite, the drug pusher and the assassin. If there are no objective, absolute values to appeal to, each individual plays by his own set of rules.

A ready answer rushes to the fore: "Ah yes, but that is where the law steps in. Laws protect us from fanaticism, preserve the common good, and maintain the social order." This is true, but it only begs the question. Laws are useful, even necessary, but even laws themselves must appeal to universal values: justice, fairness, social order, the common good. Law is not a mere convention. It upholds objective values and innate human rights.

We could push the argument to its logical conclusion. What if we allow the anti-legalist to interrogate the subjectivist: "Doesn't my opinion hold equal weight with the rest? You appreciate justice but I despise it. You can thwart me by force from doing as I please, but don't make any claim to righteousness."

If there are no absolute values, law loses all foundation; there is no standard by which to evaluate the actions of politicians, criminals, and dictators, or even the particular laws themselves. The law is just one more arbitrary value, backed up by force. It has always been true that those in power can execute their subjective will and dominate those who disagree with them. But this is the code of savages. Think of the atrocities perpetrated in France during the Revolution under the Reign of Terror. Robespierre professed to embody the *volonté générale* — the general will — but under this title he liberally slaughtered those whose views were at odds with his own.

A group of people or a law can be mistaken as easily as a single individual. A given society can vote in favor of slavery or abortion or the extermination of a segment of its population (Hitler was elected democratically) but legality doesn't guarantee these things moral legitimacy or value. Might makes right when right is viewed as nothing more than each man's fancy. Likewise, law serves the common good only when it rests on the solid groundwork of objective values.

As John Paul II perspicaciously observes in his encyclical letter *Veritatis Splendor*:

> If there is no ultimate truth to guide and direct political activity, then ideas and convictions can easily be manipulated for reasons of power. As history demonstrates, a democracy without values easily turns into open or thinly disguised totalitarianism.

HUMAN VALUES

Having established that values are essentially both objective and subjective, we can turn the focus of our attention to human values and subsequently to the different types or levels of value. What is a human value? Human values are those universal goods that pertain to our nature as persons and make us in a sense more human. They better us as persons and perfect our human nature.

Because of our freedom, we are able to ennoble our existence or impoverish it. This isn't true for the rest of creation. A tabby cat cannot become more or less a cat; it will always act in an eminently feline way, and it is not to be blamed or praised for it. But we, on the other hand, are capable of acting like a brute (and sometimes do) by obeying our lower instincts and inclinations, and in this way we become less human. The fifth-century courtier and philosopher, Boëthius, has this to say:

> Man towers above the rest of creation so long as he recognizes his own nature, and when he forgets it, he sinks lower than the beasts. For other living things to be ignorant of themselves, is natural; but for man it is a defect.

If we fail to know ourselves, our values will be correspondingly inadequate. The better we come to grips with our nature, the easier it will be to form solid values.

Of Nourishment and Nature

There is a difference between human values in general and our own personal values. The concept of human values embraces all those things that are good for us as human beings and lead to our betterment as such. Personal values are those which have been assimilated into our own life and which motivate us in our daily choices.

We could compare the difference between human values in general and personal values to the difference between certain foods and their respective worth to the human body. Nourishment is to the body what values are to the human person.

Because of the body's needs there are some foods that are conducive to good health, others that are deleterious, and others that are tolerated by the digestive system in modest quantities. We need a certain balance of vitamins, roughage, minerals, and proteins to maintain good health. This could be compared, as far as it goes, to human values, which nourish or benefit us as human beings. Thus we have an array of cultural, intellectual, and aesthetic values, all of which are beneficial for our development as human beings and round out our personality.

In the case of bodily nourishment there is also room for personal preferences. Aside from slight variations in caloric content, it makes little difference whether one eats broccoli or green beans or peas. The human organism will accept any of these and derive similar nourishment. What matters is that our diet be balanced. As long as each type of food is basically good in itself, and there is balance between the kinds of food we eat, the body receives the sustenance it needs. Similarly, our personal values are good when there is order among them and when each is good in itself.

And just as with the body there are some foods which are more beneficial and others which are added to embellish the meal, so in the case of values there is a hierarchy that favors our growth. A discreet serving of carrot cake and French vanilla ice cream makes a nice topper to end a family dinner, but we wouldn't think of eating cake and ice cream three times a day and ending with a small portion of meat and potatoes. Our organism wouldn't stand for it (nor would our waistline). Human values as well can be ordered and classified according to the benefits they provide. Some are essential, others more peripheral.

A HIERARCHY OF VALUES

Within the domain of objective values there exists a scale, a hierarchy. Not every value is the same. Some values are more important than others because they are more transcendent, because they elevate me more as a human person and correspond to my higher faculties. We can assign human values to four basic categories: (1) religious values, (2) moral values, (3) human, infra-moral values, and (4) biological values.

Religious values:	Faith, hope, charity, humility, etc.
Moral values:	Sincerity, fairness, fidelity, kindness, honesty, benevolence, etc.
Human, infra-moral values:	Prosperity, intellectual pursuits, social values, aesthetic values, success, peace of mind, etc.
Biological values:	Health, beauty, pleasure, physical strength, etc.

The lowest tier is on the biological or sensory level. Values of this level are not specific to human beings but are shared by other living organisms. It includes such concepts as health, pleasure, physical beauty and athletic qualities. Unfortunately there are persons who place much of their emphasis here. It is not uncommon to hear the phrase, "As long as I have my health, that's all that really matters." This would imply that one would be better off as a healthy mafia kingpin than an ailing saint. Or as Thomas à Kempis said some five centuries ago, "Many worry about living a long life, but few are concerned with living a good life."

Being healthy or handsome doesn't make you more a person; it doesn't increase your dignity or your worth. This is the base level, the one we share with the animals. A person like Voltaire, who at times was less concerned with exactitude than with making a point, could say that a barnyard rooster is "gallant, honest, disinterested, bearer of all virtues."

Quaint as this imagery may be, it can hardly be taken literally. You can have a healthy rabbit but you can't have a sincere rabbit. You can have a beautiful redwood tree but you can't have a redwood tree with a sense of justice. Some people spend much of their time investigating health foods, planning their diet and following an exercise program. All of this has a place in life, but a limited place, like the kick-off in a football game. Beauty, physical condition, pleasure and health are important but they don't constitute the meaning of life. We need not live to eat merely because we cannot live without eating.

Values of the second level — human, infra-moral values — are specifically *human*. They refer to the development of our nature and the talents and qualities we possess. At the same time they are less important than moral values. Some values we find at this second level are intellectual, musical, artistic, social and aesthetic pursuits. These truly ennoble us as persons and by them we tend towards the fulfillment of our potential.

The third level comprises values that are also specifically human. They are called moral or ethical values. This level is of an essentially higher rank than the others we have mentioned. This is because moral values have to do with the way we use our freedom, that sublime and incomparable gift that makes us resemble God and empowers us as authors of our own destiny. These are the human values *par excellence*, since they determine *our value as persons*. Among others, moral values include honesty, kindness, justice, authenticity, solidarity, sincerity, and mercy.

While at times the lower values are mutually exclusive (it is difficult to paint with watercolors and play the saxophone at the same time), moral values never enter into conflict with one another. They form an organic whole. We can, and should, be sincere, just, honest and upright all at the same time. Each supports and sustains the others and together they form a sound, solid structure which is the personality of a mature person.

Moral values are unconditional and always prevail over lower values. I cannot sacrifice justice to enjoy greater prosperity, or forego loyalty to a friend in order to be thought well of. This isn't always the case between the two lower levels. Although music is a higher value than food, at times I have to get up from playing the saxophone to take a bite to eat.

There is also a fourth and highest level of values which builds upon and completes the values of the third level, and even permits us to transcend our nature. These are religious values. Religious values have to do with our personal relationship with God.

There is a simple fact that modern society often overlooks: the human person is religious. Although we are unlikely to read this in any sociology textbook (the founder of sociology, Auguste Comte, was adamantly anti-religious and believed that religion had been effectively replaced by science), there has been no society in history without religion. We naturally long for God because we were made for Him.

In 1991 *U.S. News & World Report* published the results of a random survey among Americans. The question read: "What is the most important goal in your life?" 56% of those interviewed responded: "A closer relationship with God." By our very nature we are religious. Whether we always realize it or not, we need God.

As Pope John Paul II reflects in his book *Crossing the Threshold of Hope*, the question of God's existence touches the very heart of man's search for meaning:

> One clearly sees that the response to the question *An Deus sit* (whether God exists) is not only an issue that touches the intellect; it is, at the same time, an issue that has a strong impact on all of human existence. It depends on a multitude of situations in which man searches for the significance and the meaning of his own existence. Questioning God's existence is intimately united *with the purpose of human existence.*

We naturally look for transcendence. We were made to go beyond ourselves, to tend upward towards the absolute. St. Augustine expresses this truth on the very first page of his *Confessions* when he says: "You have made us for yourself, O Lord, and our hearts are restless until they rest in you." The reality of our transcendence as human beings is what gives sense and meaning to our life on earth. We eagerly cultivate religious values because they correspond to the truth of our existence.

God *is* the ultimate and supreme value for all human beings. Not just for me, not just for you, but for everyone. In this very real sense, we all have the same destiny, just as we all share the same human nature.

A CHRISTIAN PERSPECTIVE

What relationship do values have with Christianity? If human values depend on what is good for us as human beings, in what way do our values as Christians differ from those of a non-Christian? Finally, why are we concerned with human values at all? Aren't religious values enough?

There are three main reasons for us as Christians to study and reflect on human values. First, a Christian is a human person, a member of the human family. Everything that is truly good for humanity is equally good for the Christian. Christianity elevates us but doesn't change our nature.

Secondly, God Himself became one of us to reveal to us the truth about human existence. Jesus Christ is God, but He is also man. If in Him we know God, we also know ourselves — the ideal human being, the perfect person. Christians are deeply concerned about human life because God is deeply concerned about it. If we want to know what it means to be truly human and what things are important in life, we discover these things in our Lord's own life.

Finally, even if we hold that all that really matters is holiness, we should recognize that holiness is not something abstract and disconnected from our daily existence. Our human activity is warp and woof of our relationship with God, and a solid scale of values is the essential infrastructure of a life of holiness. First the human being, then the saint. Grace builds on nature. Holiness supposes an interior harmony, a well-formed character, and a clear idea of what is important in life and what isn't.

Jesus often spoke about priorities, and His own life is a transparent testimony of where true values lie. The essence of His teaching on values is the relative unimportance of material well-being as compared with eternal life. "What does it profit a man if he gains the whole world and loses his soul? What can a man offer in exchange for his soul?" (Mt 16:26). Everything else in this world comes to an end: cars, clothes, youth, beauty, friends, pleasure, learning — everything but God. At the end of life all that remains is what we have done for God and for others.

This emphasis on the relative value of temporal goods as compared to eternal ones is repeated time and time again in Christ's parables. He encourages His followers to keep their sights fixed on Heaven and not to get bogged down in fleeting pleasures and riches that the world has to offer. Another such example of Christ's lucid scale of values can be found in St. Luke's Gospel:

> Do not worry about your lives and what you are to eat or your bodies and how you are to clothe them, because life means more than food and the body more than clothing. Look at the ravens: they do not sow or reap, they have no barns, yet God feeds them. And how much more are you worth than the birds! [. . .] But you, you must not set your hearts on things to eat or things to drink; nor must you worry. It is the pagans of this world who set their hearts on all these things. Your Father well knows you need them. No; set your hearts on His Kingdom, and these other things will be given you as well (Lk 12:22-31).

Jesus also differentiates the value of our actions. For example, when a poor widow contributes two copper coins to the Temple treasury, Christ assures those around Him that her gift had more worth than the prodigious donations of the rich. "Because these gave from their surplus, but she from the little she had, has put in everything she possessed, all she had to live on" (Mk 12:44). On the other hand He upbraids the Pharisees for having flipped the scale of values upside down. They wash the outside of cups and dishes, and neglect the more important matters of the law: "justice, mercy, good faith" (Mt 22:23).

When asked which of the laws is the most important, He does not hesitate to highlight love of God and love of neighbor as the sum and substance of the law, far more important than any burnt offering.

St. Paul, too, exhorts the members of the early Church to conserve this scale of values, to become "new men" with a new set of criteria and values. These values should distinguish the Christian from the non-believer. In one passage he says:

> And so if you have risen with Christ, seek the things that are above, where Christ is seated at God's right hand. Aspire to heavenly things, not to the things of the earth (Col 3:1-2).

And when addressing himself to the Corinthians, he offers a similar message:

> We have no eyes for things that are visible, but only for things that are invisible; for visible things last only for a time, and the invisible things are eternal (2 Cor 4:18).

Christianity offers a global vision of human existence, a way of seeing and evaluating all the events and activities of human life. This vision is based on the truth about what it means to be human, about our final destiny and about our relationship with God and with the world. Values deal with what is *good*, and the surest way to know what is *good* for us as human beings is to know *who* we are. This will be the topic of the following chapter.

CHAPTER 2

THE FOUNDATION
OF VALUE

Perhaps you are familiar with the story of the eagle that grew up in the hen house. An eagle egg was found one day and placed in a chicken coop to see if it would hatch. When it did the young eagle adapted to the poultry world, learning to behave like a chicken.

One day a fellow eagle spotted him in the chicken yard and flew down to exchange a few words with him. "What are you doing here, with your beak in the mud? You were made for greater things: to soar about the heavens, to be a master hunter, to contemplate the earth from far, far above."

Finally one day the other eagle convinced him to at least try, to watch him take off and land, and to test the capability of his own wings. In this way, the eagle learned to fly.

The moral of the tale is easy to identify: *the heights we reach depend on the ideals we set for ourselves and the degree to which we live up to our potential.* To set our goals we must first have an idea of what we are capable of. One of the biggest helps in establishing our values will be understanding our nature.

We have said that a value is a good, recognized and appreciated as a good. But what is good for us as human beings? To get to the root of human values, we need to leave aside personal idiosyncrasies in order to focus on our *common* nature. We are looking for things that are *universally* good for us.

A good is that which improves or perfects. Something is good for us if it makes us *better* persons. This can happen in two ways: either according to our nature, or according to our purpose or end. That is, something is good for me according to *what I am* (i.e. it helps me to be what I am meant to be) or according to *what I am for* (i.e. it helps me to *achieve* the purpose of my existence). This distinction will allow us to unearth the substructure of human values.

NATURE

We all know that an internal combustion engine doesn't run well on milk, whereas a kitten does. This is because they have fundamentally different constitutions or natures. What's good for the goose is good for the gander because a goose and gander share the same nature. What's good for the goose is not necessarily good for the ostrich, the meadowlark or the scarlet tanager.

Similarly, because of its nature, it is good for a tree to prune it, to water it, and to fertilize it with manure. Not all creatures, however, would benefit from the amputation of their members, and many would object to being encircled in organic fertilizer. We need to know what something *is* before we know what is *good* for it.

Lassie, Benji and Snoopy are three distinct individuals, but there is something they share which makes them all dogs. This is their nature. The nature of something is simply what it is. A cow has a bovine nature, a wolf has a lupine nature, and a human being has a human nature. *Nature is what we are.*

Despite our many differences we share a common nature. We have certain qualities that identify us as human persons and distinguish us from all other beings. For example, you and I have different personalities but we both have a personality. An adobe brick has no personality. You may be much more intelligent than I am, but we both have an intellect. Geraniums have no intellect. You and I are both concrete, individual, distinct realizations of human nature. Therefore human nature doesn't preclude individuality. Each person is really and truly unique, individual, and priceless. Yet each one is first of all a human being.

There are several special characteristics of our nature that radically separate us from the rest of creation. These traits will lead us to discover the foundation for our common human values. But before examining them in detail, let us consider the other dimension of goodness.

FINALITY OR PURPOSE

Certain things are good for us because they help us attain our end or purpose. If we can ascertain where we are going as human beings, what our purpose is, then we can also know what is good for us in this sense.

This is easy enough to see on the level of our personal goals. The svelte 105-pound gymnast who specializes in the uneven bars wouldn't think of eating the eight raw eggs and stack of pancakes that the 300-pound Dallas Cowboy lineman routinely packs away for breakfast. Because of her objective to be an Olympic-class gymnast, certain things become good for her. They are good because they help her achieve her goal.

We can apply this same principle to the human person in general. In this context, it is a question of focusing not on our individual goals, but on the universal purpose and destiny of us all. Once again, we should remember that each of us has a specific, unique destiny and purpose in life. At the same time, we have a common purpose that derives from our common nature. True values help us to accomplish this purpose.

THE FOUNDATION OF VALUE

The human person is a mystery. A mystery that all of us, to some degree, try to unravel. What is man? Who am I? Our interest in this question is not a matter of mere academic curiosity, nor even a legitimate desire to know more about ourselves. Our concern here is the objective basis of human values. In dealing with values, we find that an investigation of human nature is the key to discovering our true good. We cannot hope to know what is good for us until we have confronted the problem of who we are.

A quick tour through human history can leave us shaking our heads in wonder. The human being. . . so great and yet so incredibly frail. Able to effect colossal projects, yet also capable of the basest and most heinous iniquity. Is it possible that Joseph Stalin, St. Francis of Assisi, Nero and Mother Teresa of Calcutta all belong to the same human race?

Our awe before the nobility and the misery of our human race is mirrored in the words of the Psalmist: "What is man that You should spare a thought for him, or the son of man that You should care for him? Yet You have made him little less than the angels, crowning him with glory and splendor" (Ps 8:5-6). Shakespeare's words, too, echo the spontaneous admiration and wonder that we experience when we come face to face with the marvel of man:

> What a piece of work is man! How noble in reason! How infinite in faculty! In form and moving how express and admirable! In action how like an angel! In apprehension how like a god! the paragon of animals! And yet, to me, what is this quintessence of dust? (*Hamlet*, ii, 2).

Where can we look for answers to the enigma surrounding our human nature? Nowadays most products come with instructions on the package. We are told what ingredients are contained in the food we eat, in what dosage and under what circumstances we are to take our medicine, and what washing procedure is most effective for the garments we buy. A newborn baby, however, comes into the world naked and fully assembled, with no instruction labels or owner's manual. To know what a person is, and thus what is good for him or her, we must look elsewhere.

There are two chief sources that let us know who we are: experience and divine revelation. Experience is continual observation and first-hand contact with ourselves and with other persons. Our nature is shown through our actions, through our abilities, and through our innate tendencies. We reflect on our own actions and motivations by the power of our intelligence and we discover many significant things about who we are.

At the same time there are many secrets and mysteries which go beyond our experience, but which we know through the gift of divine revelation. In the person of Jesus Christ the mystery of the human person is disclosed to us. Revelation is like a divine designer's manual. God, Who knows us inside and out, has not left us in the dark as to who we are and where we are going. He has clued us in to the divine plan and given us operating and care instructions.

It's a good thing He did, since many enigmas of our existence such as death, suffering, and the ultimate meaning of life are beyond the reach of simple observation.

WHO IS MAN?

If we draw on these two sources — reason and revelation — we can distinguish four fundamental characteristics of our human nature. These give a clear picture of who we are at the heart of our being. We are (1) creatures, (2) made in the image and likeness of God (rational and free), (3) composed of body and soul, (4) with a nature wounded by original sin.

First of all, we are *creatures*. By creatures we don't mean one of those nasty green lizard things that emerge from the black lagoon to prey on innocent townspeople. A creature is simply what is created. You and I haven't always existed; nor have human beings as a species. This isn't the place to go into a discussion of creationist or evolutionary theories. The *mode* in which God created the first human beings is less important than the *fact* that He did indeed create them.

Our creaturehood carries with it some interesting corollaries. To begin with, we find that we are fundamentally dependent, intrinsically dependent on God, our Creator. We modern men and women often like to think that we are wholly autonomous and able to take care of ourselves. That is true up to a point, but at the very origin of our being is the fact of our creation. We depend on Another to bring us into existence and to sustain us in existence. This is what we share with every other creature: with stones, minerals, shrubs, animals, fish, comets and angels. We do not come from ourselves but from God.

Secondly, we are *rational* and *free*. There is something totally unique about our creation: we are created in God's image and likeness. We reflect God in a way that no other creature does. God created us in His own image, "male and female He created them" we read in the book of Genesis (1:27). As Chesterton wrote, "Man is not merely an evolution but rather a revolution." Human beings are a revolution because they are radically different from the rest of creation, the only creatures God made for Himself.

We may not always act rationally, but by nature we have the capacity to think and to know. We are *rational* beings. This quality is, in fact, the one that makes us like God and separates us from the whole world of other living creatures. It also grants us the dignity of personhood. We are not things, but persons. I am not a "something," but a "someone."

Because we are rational, we are also *free*. This quality, which opens up a world of possibilities and confers on us a dignity above all non-rational creatures, derives from the spiritual dimension of our nature. We reflect, ponder, deliberate and act. We plan and program for the future.

Freedom is not only a value in itself, but also the necessary condition that allows us to form values. If we were pre-programmed and obliged to follow our instincts the way the animals are, "value" would be a meaningless word. As it is, we are able to recognize values and are free to pursue them.

Thirdly, we are persons with a *body* and a *soul*. These aren't two distinct parts that are artificially joined, but two essential dimensions of our one human nature. We are a unity. We aren't spirits imprisoned or entombed in a body, as Plato believed. Nor are we the composition of two different substances — one material and the other immaterial, as Descartes considered us. You and I don't *have* a body and soul; we *are* body and soul.

Because of this duality present in our nature, we are linked with the material world and with the spiritual world. We have some things in common with plants and animals, and in other things we resemble the angels. This concept is crucial, because it helps us to understand that we are more than just organic matter; therefore, our values will go beyond what is merely good for our body or pleasing to our senses.

Finally, our nature is wounded, warped by original sin. Our personal experience testifies to a certain division that exists within us. This explains why it is often difficult to do what is right, even when we know what is right. Often our body tells us one thing, and our reason advises us to do the contrary. Doing what is right doesn't come easy, and we have to work to overcome and master our tendencies. "God and the devil are fighting there and the battlefield is the heart," Dostoyevsky says in *The Brothers Karamazov*.

This internal fissure at the core of our being is another key aspect of our nature and throws light on the cause of many of our difficulties. By coming to grips with this fact, however, we discover that an important value for us as human beings is the regaining of harmony in our being. We need to master ourselves and organize our faculties according to a proper hierarchy.

These four characteristics of human nature provide the key for understanding what is good for us as persons created in the image and likeness of God with intellect and free will, a body and a soul and a nature wounded by sin. But this description is only partial. We still must look at the other dimension of our being: our purpose or destiny.

THE MEANING OF LIFE

Life is full of *purpose*. The thousand and one episodes that make up our existence fit together in a bigger picture. Life is not a disconnected series of experiences and sensations, but a story; life is not a state of being but a journey. Why are we here? Where are we going? Here we can consider three interrelated answers.

God made us to know Him, love Him, and serve Him in this life so as to be eternally happy with Him in Heaven. Of all the visible creatures on earth only we are capable of knowing and loving our Creator. Knowing and loving God is what we are here to do; it is the meaning and purpose of our life on earth.

It is easy to miss the boat and think that loving God is just one aspect of life, another category along with water-skiing, a day at the office and going to the movies. This is not the case. All our activities fit into the larger scheme of the true meaning of life: knowing and loving God. This isn't an occupation or an activity alongside others; it is the framework and intimate motivation within which we do everything we do.

A second, complementary answer to our destiny is our *mortality*. Each and every one of us will one day die. This isn't a morbid thought, fit only for the likes of Edgar Allan Poe and Stephen King. Death is real and important and worthy of consideration.

Evidently there are many ways of looking at this reality. The German philosopher Martin Heidegger would say that we are "a being towards death." The Epicureans who lived around the time of Christ followed the motto: "Eat, drink, and be merry, for tomorrow we shall die." Our view of death will greatly condition our view of life and, consequently, our view of what contributes to our ultimate good. If death were truly the end of our existence, our life on earth would be absurd.

Fortunately, death is not the end of existence but the gateway to new life. We are made for an eternal happiness which is unattainable in this life, and of which earthly joy is just a faint reflection and foretaste. Next to eternity, life is but the blink of an eye. From this perspective we can understand the centuries-old maxim that offers us a standard to evaluate all things: *Quid hoc ad aeternitatem?* (How does this relate to eternity?). Things that pass away with time can never have the same worth as what lasts forever.

A final characteristic of our human destiny is the reality of *judgment*. Our death is not the ultimate reality, but neither are life on earth and life after death two unconnected facts. Our life here affects and even determines the state of our existence after death.

Sir Isaac Newton assures us that on earth there is no physical action that does not produce an effect. Each of our moral actions also produces its effect. There are eternal consequences of every act, every good or bad example, every kind word. We are responsible for our choices and one day we will render an account for them. Jesus speaks of Heaven as a reward, and Hell as a punishment.

The consideration of judgment as something that awaits all of us after death offers us still more material from which to examine our ultimate good. A football player values certain exercises and drills in practice that appear to be worth little in themselves. Those drills form part of the big picture and prepare him for the moment of truth in the game on Sunday. He is what he is on Sunday, because he did what he did from Monday to Saturday. Our true good here and now is what can be considered good from the perspective of eternity.

KEEPING SHIPSHAPE

Besides examining the essential characteristics of our human nature and destiny, it is useful to take stock of the tools we have at hand to accomplish our goals, that is, our qualities, talents and capabilities. A good inventory of our interior world will be a significant asset in our quest to be men and women of solid values.

What instruments do we have at our disposal to achieve our objectives? We — union of material body and spiritual soul — possess certain powers or faculties. A *faculty* is simply the capability to carry out a particular type of action.

If we observe a car going up a hill, we can be sure that there is a motor inside. Every action requires a capacity, the power to bring it about. If you and I can see, it follows that we must have the faculty of sight. If we can think and reason, we must necessarily have the *power* to think. This power is the faculty of intelligence. We become aware of our faculties by observing our own actions and the actions of others.

Not all faculties are on the same level. The ability to smell is definitely not as sublime as the ability to reason. Since we are a unity, all our faculties work together and all are important, but they work together according to a certain order.

An illustrative (albeit limited) analogy is that of a sailing vessel. Each of us is like a ship on a voyage across the ocean. The instruments and crew of the ship as well as the circumstances of sailing all come into play in our voyage through life. The parts of a sailing ship work together so that the vessel can function properly. Each part has its particular purpose.

Passions

A first element to be taken into account is our passions. They urge us on to action as the winds that fill a ship's sails drive it forward. Sometimes winds are as strong as a gale or a monsoon and propel the ship with incredible force. At other times they are gentler and allow the vessel to move ahead with serenity.

Often we do not want to go in the same direction as the wind is blowing. That is, while some passions are positive, others pull us off course and urge us in a different direction from the route we have plotted.

Passions are strong, natural tendencies that drive us toward or away from something. In themselves they are neither good nor bad — just like the wind. It all depends on whether they assist or impede us in our journey. There are bodily passions (sexual desire, appetite, comfort, and so forth) and passions of the spirit (love, ambition, fear, pride, envy, anger). Some theorists have proposed the notion that it is unhealthy to control our passions and that we would be better off if we were to give them free rein. Freudians, for example, advocate yielding to our instinctual impulses as a necessary means "to live in accordance with our psychological truth."

It is, however, precisely in the mastery of reason over instinct where we show ourselves to be superior to animals and reach our true dignity. *Channeling* our passions is not the same as *repressing* them. When I feel hungry at 5:00 in the afternoon, there is no sense in trying to convince myself that I am not really hungry. A sensible response would be to keep going another hour until dinner time, instead of leaving my desk in an instinctual search for the nearest refrigerator. We need to harness the energy of our passions and direct them toward our goals.

Feelings

A second force at work in us is that of our feelings, which can be compared to the sea's current. The current can also be helpful or harmful. Sometimes it crosses our course or pulls the ship toward dangerous shoals. At other times it is right in line with our desired bearing and gives an added boost in the right direction.

Our feelings act in the same way. Sometimes I feel like doing what I know I should do. At other times my feelings are an obstacle to the accomplishment of my objectives. Feelings are personal, purely subjective, spontaneous, psychological reactions to stimuli. Since they are reactions, they are blind, passive and outside our control. We can't just decide to feel happy or sad, excited or down in the dumps.

An important thing to take into account in dealing with our feelings is that they are *nonrational*: they don't always correspond to our true good. Therefore we must sometimes go against them. If the captain allows his sailing vessel to drift with the current, he is headed for eventual shipwreck.

Personality Type

A third factor to consider is our personality type, a dimension of our character that we are born with. Personality type (or temperament) is like the *model* of ship we're sailing. There are canoes, rowboats, small sailboats, and larger craft, such as schooners or large ocean liners. Some craft are sleek, lightweight and maneuverable, like a catamaran. Others are slow but steady, seaworthy and durable.

Our temperament is the sum-total of our natural tendencies and dispositions. Some people are naturally optimistic, outgoing, frank and sincere. Others are more introverted, pensive and sentimental. Some individuals are active, others passive. Some tend to be more emotional, others less.

The important thing here is to know ourselves well so as to work with our particular temperament and use it to our advantage. From this raw material we form our character. The captain has to take into account what type of vessel he is sailing, its peculiarities, drawbacks and strong points. In this way he will be able to reach his destination.

Intelligence

These three elements — passions, feelings, and temperament — are part of our bodily nature. We also have two spiritual faculties: our intelligence and our will. Both of these faculties come into play in the pursuit of values; *intelligence* recognizes what is good and the *will* chooses it. The object of intelligence is truth, reality, the way things are. It is our capability to reflect, to reason, to contemplate, to analyze and synthesize.

"All men desire to know," as Aristotle assures us. We are naturally interested in the way things are, and why they are the way they are. Our intelligence is never satisfied, never full, but always open to more, to the infinite.

Intelligence is like the ship's captain who analyzes the vessel's course and gives directions to the helmsman. The captain doesn't work alone but is aided by the lookout in the crow's nest (*five senses*), his compass (*conscience*) and his many charts and maps (*faith*).

The lookout is the eyes of the ship and informs the captain of the presence of rocks, shallow waters, barrier reefs, storms and land. He is alert to changing situations. In a similar way, the human person receives information about the outside world through the *five senses*: sight, smell, taste, touch and hearing.

A ship's compass lets the captain know which way is true north so he can adjust the vessel's bearing. Likewise our *conscience* keeps our life on course and offers us a sure guide.

The charts and maps he has at his disposal inform him with certainty about things that have not yet appeared on the horizon. There are rocks he cannot see, perilous straits to be avoided, shortcuts to be taken advantage of. In like manner, our *faith* provides us with certainty about things which surpass our personal experience or the limitations of empirical knowledge.

Will

The last component of our ship is the helmsman. In the last analysis he is the one who determines where the ship will go. This role corresponds to the human will. Even when there are adverse winds, waves and currents, a good helmsman is able to keep the vessel on course and channel the other forces toward his chosen heading.

On the human plane, a person is worth what his will is worth. Will is the backbone of character. Thus a person of character is a person of willpower. If we think of the greatest achievers in history and even the greatest men and women of our own time, we find that willpower is never lacking.

There have been great leaders and great saints who weren't very intelligent (the Curé of Ars comes to mind), but there is no such thing as a leader or saint without willpower. We can even say that a person becomes *more* a person through the dominion of his intelligence and will over his lower tendencies. Our passions drive us, our external senses offer us data, but whether we act as free men or not depends on the strength of our will.

This, then, in a nutshell, is a summary of our faculties and some of the forces at work within each of us. A fundamental value for us as persons is the proper *ordering* of our faculties. Just as a sports team's success depends on the coordination and mutual support of the individual members, so too the coordination of these powers in the human person is the groundwork for all other values.

To form authentic values, it is important to take these different dimensions of our human nature into account. Understanding who we are and what we are made for is critical for choosing good values — those which will aid us in our life's work.

Of the different qualities mentioned, one stands out as particularly important in a discussion of values: human freedom. Seeking after good values, choosing them and living in accord with them all presuppose freedom.

This is such an important and misunderstood topic, that it merits an entire chapter.

CHAPTER 3

FREEDOM AND VALUES

Few values possess such universal appeal as freedom. The word is bandied about like a badminton birdie and provides the ostensible foundation for entities as diverse as political parties, day-care centers, the ACLU and the Marines. The protagonists of the French Revolution adopted freedom as one of the foundation stones of their creed: *Liberté! Egalité! Fraternité!* Several years earlier the American colonial revolutionaries had taken up arms against Britain under the same banner, summed up in Patrick Henry's famous "Give me liberty or give me death!" Freedom is an ideal that seems never to go out of fashion. It's hard to find a revolutionary campaign or national constitution that doesn't espouse freedom as one of its basic tenets.

Today with the demise of Communism, the spread of democracy, the availability of information and the apparently limitless advances of technology, the human race is experiencing an acute sense of freedom. Western culture pays homage to liberty in every social sector. We have statues and space shuttles that bear her name, coins minted in her honor, shampoos and toothpaste that promise to somehow increase our personal freedom if we purchase them.

The word *freedom* has an almost magical ring to it. There are certain words that carry a sort of positive or negative charge, like ions. Words like "choice," "creativity," "new," "original," and "freedom" bear a positive charge: we are already favorably disposed to them before we even know what they refer to. Other words often produce aversion, and from the outset taint our reaction to what is being said. If we are to be objective, we must sift through the emotional impact to consider the real value behind the expression.

Take the words "new" and "original." The fact that an idea is new or original tells us practically nothing about it, and we don't have a clue if it is a worthwhile idea or a ridiculous one. It sometimes happens that the new is inferior to the old. Think of what happened when the "new Coke" came out. It caught on like a forest fire till people realized the "old Coke" was better. Or consider the word "choice," another word with appeal but in reality an ambiguous value. What really matters are the concrete *choices* we make and not abstract *choice*.

THE MANY FACES OF FREEDOM

The same principle applies to the concept of freedom or liberty. It is an analogous term, used in multifarious ways. A certain lioness named Elsa was "born free" — that is, was never meant for captivity. It is said that there's no such thing as a "free lunch" — that is, with no strings attached. A "free bird" is not in a cage. A "salt-free" diet is marked by the lack of this presumably pernicious substance. Then, too, we have the case of the well-oiled door that swings "freely" on its hinges, or the mother of six who finally has some "free time" on her hands when the last little cherub marches off to kindergarten.

In some instances freedom can simply refer to the absence of some offensive element, and is the approximate equivalent of the suffix *-less*. For example, sugar-free = sugarless, trouble free = the absence of trouble. But in this sense, freedom is really neither here nor there. While it retains its inherent appeal, its worth depends directly on the undesirability of that which is absent. Caffeine-free is a positive attribute when caffeine is held to be unappealing. On the other hand, who would go to a fun-free amusement park? Ever try swimming in a water-free pool?

When Pope John Paul II speaks of freedom as the root of all human dignity, he is referring to a profound reality that goes far beyond mere freedom of movement or the absence of external constraint. Specifically human freedom is an essential part of man's nature and separates him in a radical way from the rest of creation. Human beings are essentially free even when they're in a cage or slaving away in a forced-labor camp; an animal isn't free even when soaring through the air or roaming unrestrained about the Serengeti Plain. Nature itself is not free but obeys a series of fixed laws. Water always runs downhill. A fire can't be ignited in a vacuum. The combination of sodium and chlorine may produce salt, but it will never give us pepper.

Human freedom is not intellectual or physical freedom, but freedom of the will — or free will — by which we govern our own actions. A human act is a free act.

Strictly speaking, it is not the same to say "actions of a human being" and "human actions." A *human act* is that which is human in the full sense of the word: performed with consciousness and liberty. Sometimes our actions are deliberate and fully conscious, other times we act inadvertently or even do things involuntarily. When the checkout clerk at the pharmacy accidentally hands Bob twice the change due to him, she has not performed a human act because it was not intentional. When on arriving to his car Bob realizes her error and goes back to return what isn't rightfully his, he *has* performed a human act because it was conscious and free.

Human liberty includes moral freedom, and allows for the possibility of good and evil, virtue and vice. Your act of kindness to a small child has value and merit because it is a free act. Liberty is not like a math test where we "choose" the correct answers — a computer could "choose" them just as well (or better). Nor is it simply spontaneity, choosing between different a-moral possibilities as a mother bird does when she "chooses" in which tree and on which branch to build her nest. Human liberty finds its full expression in the choice between different good things, and between good and evil.

THREE LEVELS OF FREEDOM

Since freedom is a word with many meanings, it is necessary to distinguish and clarify the different dimensions of freedom.

Freedom From

This application of freedom refers to the condition of being unfettered and without external interference in one's personal activity. The term freedom is most commonly used in this sense. It is *autonomy* as opposed to *outside control.* A teenager may seek more freedom from his or her parents. Industries look for freedom from governmental restrictions. The prison inmate longs for the day when he will taste freedom once again. And yet this liberty, which is good in itself, can be misused. When a person seeks freedom from responsibility or freedom from all commitment, he is making a grave mistake, since he is trying to avoid necessary ingredients of his fulfillment as a human being.

Another danger of this aspect of freedom is the possibility of being manipulated, where one believes it is he who decides whereas in reality it is another. We could ask whether people are more or less free today than in the past. Surely they are more mobile. They also have more advanced means of instantaneous communication and information processing. They have a greater control over their environment and are able to do things that people in the past could only dream of.

Yet on a personal level they often find themselves confused, unsure, unable to think for themselves and to escape the barrage of noise, images and subtle messages generated by society and particularly by the mass media. Their principles are attacked and they find little support in trying to live as authentic human beings. Consequently, in practice many of their actions, choices and preferences are defined for them by fashion, public opinion and political correctness. This manipulation often comes about through a direct appeal to the emotions, and bypasses the process of rational choice.

To ensure our freedom we must defend our independence from such external pressures.

Freedom To

You are the author of your actions. When you go to the grocery store or speak with your neighbor or visit a friend in the hospital, you are exercising your freedom in a series of conscious acts. Right now, you and I are freely writing our own history. This dimension of freedom is *possibility*, as opposed to *necessity*. Necessity is that which couldn't be otherwise. Human actions are never subject to necessity, because every truly human action is a free action. Persons are free. Things are necessary. Seen in this light freedom is the degree to which a subject's actions depend on the subject himself.

Besides our actions, we are also free to be the type of people we choose to be. An honest person is honest by *choice*, not by *compulsion*. Here we are referring to *self-determination*, as opposed to *determinism*. Nowadays — as in the past — we come across people who deny free will, claiming that the human person is conditioned, incapable of free choice. Some assert a biological determinism — our decisions are already present in our genes. Others speak of cultural and social conditioning that determines our way of thinking and choosing.

There is a modest dosage of truth in both these positions. We are, indeed, affected by bio-logical and social factors. But in the final analysis we are free beings, and despite outside influences our decisions are our own. It would be easier to blame someone else for our failings, but we know that ultimately the responsibility is ours. In the same light, good actions deserve praise, because in the face of different possibilities, goodness was freely chosen.

Freedom is not just desire. It is the ability to carry out that desire. You can want to never die or wish you were seven feet tall, but you can't choose these because you lack the power to bring them about. We can only choose those things whose performance lies within our capabilities.

Freedom For

True liberation is more than clearing away rubble from life's runway or removing the chains that hold us captive. We clear the runway in order to take off in a plane. We unchain a person so that he can live out his life, fulfill his dreams. We seek to be *free from* constraints so that we can be *free for* action. Freedom suggests activity, a desired goal. "I'm free Friday night" already implies that I'm free for something — it is understood that there is something we want to accomplish.

Freedom begs for commitment, for realization. If I'm free on Friday night but wind up doing nothing, I stay home like a hen sitting on her roost waiting for something to hatch. Finally I have a couple hours free so I can. . . work on that model airplane, finish that book, write Aunt Sarah. This aspect of freedom is *decision* and *activity*, as opposed to *indecision* and *passivity*. Freedom is freedom when it is actualized, when it is exercised.

On this level the opposite of freedom is passivity and non-commitment. Nowadays there is a widespread fear of commitment. Many decide not to decide because they are afraid of choosing badly. Such persons wind up as prisoners of their own insecurity and fear with regard to the future. By desperately trying to leave all their options open, they effectively close themselves off from their full realization as human persons. They want to have their cake and eat it too, without sacrificing anything. The modern syllogism of non-commitment could be stated something like this:

1. The most important thing is to be free.
2. If I exercise my freedom (commit myself) I will limit my options and become less free.
3. Therefore, I will not commit myself.

Human freedom is not the absence of commitment but the ability to commit oneself and persevere in that commitment. We realize or fulfill ourselves in the free commitment of our person and the free living out of the commitments we have undertaken. Has Judy, mother of four, lost the freedom she once had? Has Jack, swinging bachelor at 43, discovered the key to perpetual freedom? Obviously not. As we shall see, we do not find fulfillment or self-realization by disconnecting ourselves from other people or by avoiding all bonds of love, friendship and responsibility. It is precisely in this self-giving that we are actualized and fulfill our human potential.

THE VALUE OF LIBERTY

Today freedom is often understood in terms of total autonomy. It is seen as the sole and indisputable basis for personal choices and as self-affirmation at any cost. Some, such as Jean-Paul Sartre, believe that values are created by our liberty, and that liberty itself is the supreme value. This theory contains two implicit contradictions. First of all, Sartre proposes freedom as an absolute value while also maintaining that all values are relative. Secondly, the individual is held to be the creator of all values, and at the same time freedom itself must be the highest value for all. Anyone who disagrees with him is obviously mistaken. As always, relativism infallibly degenerates into dogmatism.

A further distinction is in order. It is important to differentiate between the quality of being free, and the right use of freedom. We rightly appreciate freedom in itself and recognize that it is good to be free. Freedom ennobles us as human beings and allows us to participate in a certain way in God's own freedom. But freedom can also be abused. This is why there are laws and police and prisons because of the very real possibility of the misuse of personal freedom. At a given point these institutions step in and say, "Sorry, pal, you've gone too far. You've overstepped your limits."

It's strange to see how the same concept is appealed to as the source and inspiration for conflicting activities. Sinners sin in the name of freedom and saints exercise their holiness under the same flag. Charles Manson was able to brutally murder a number of innocent persons because he was free. For the same reason Joan of Arc gave up her life rather than deny the mission she had received from God. Indeed there can be no sin, no crime, and no violence without freedom, just as there can be no sanctity, no virtue, no kindness, and no love.

But freedom is not the *inspiration* of hateful crimes, nor of great deeds of virtue. It is only the *necessary condition* which makes these actions possible. When freedom is seen as an absolute, unbounded by principles, it can lead to the gravest abuses. As Pope John Paul II said in an address he gave in Poland in January, 1993, "Freedom understood as arbitrary, separated from truth and goodness, freedom separated from God's commandments, becomes a threat to man, and leads to slavery; it turns against the individual and society."

Freedom looks to values. It provides the *possibility* to act, whereas values are my reason or *motive* for acting. If I am totally free but lack values, what will I do? My freedom won't tell me. It will only respond, "You can do anything." My values are what move me, what tell me, "Do this. It is good; it is right; it is important." Values are what attract my will; freedom is what permits my will to move towards those values. My will desires and, because it is free, it is able to pursue its desires.

It is also useful to distinguish between liberty and rights. Freedom is not some sort of cosmic rubber stamp certifying that all my actions are good and licit as long as they are done freely. Freedom is not the same as the *right* to do something, though the two are often confused. "I can do as I please! This is a free country!" To be free to do something (without constraint) does not give me the right to do it. I am *free* to kill another person (perhaps no one will physically prevent me), but I have no *right* to kill.

Freedom in itself is not a justification for anything. Tony tells his brother, "Ray, you shouldn't commit adultery. You should be faithful to your wife." Ray responds, "I can do as I please! I'm a free person." His reply misses the mark and really has little to do with Tony's fraternal admonition. No one is calling into question Ray's capability of doing such and such an action. We are all of us capable of acting like monsters, but we shouldn't act like monsters and we have no right to do so.

ODD BEDFELLOWS?

Freedom and Responsibility

Freedom carries with it some unusual corollaries. To begin with, we have the duo of freedom and responsibility. To the modern mind they seem to contradict each other, yet they are intimately united. They are not two separate realities but two aspects of the selfsame reality. Like a mother and child they are never found apart. You cannot say, "I'd like to be a mother, but without children." Its a logical impossibility. Likewise there is no freedom without responsibility — and no responsibility without freedom. Viktor Frankl once remarked that the good work begun with the Statue of Liberty in New York ought to be completed by erecting the Statue of Responsibility in Los Angeles.

The very fact that we are free means that we

are responsible for our actions. The credit or blame due to our actions falls on our own shoulders. Likewise, there is no responsibility where there is no freedom. We don't punish a tree for not moving out of the way when we drive into it. We recognize that the tree has no responsibility because it is not free. Responsibility presupposes the power to perform. I can be responsible for an action only if it is truly *mine*.

To be responsible is to "respond," to "render an account" for our actions to another to whom we are at least implicitly committed (to God, other people, our own conscience). Responsibility also means bearing the *consequences* of our actions. Often we'd like to separate the two, enjoy the benefits of freedom with none of the responsibility. This is one of the reasons why people rebel against authority, why adolescents seek independence from their parents, why certain psychologists invent methods to try to escape or explain away the persistent voice of conscience. But this divorce of freedom from responsibility would effectively destroy freedom itself. Freedom without responsibility is not freedom at all but license. To be free is to be the cause of my actions, and to be the cause is to be responsible.

Freedom and Limitation

Despite our greatness as creatures made in the image and likeness of God, we are limited beings. We learn more and more about nature and how to harness the powers of the cosmos, yet many things remain outside our control. Human freedom is not infinite or absolute. We must work within our nature. This fundamental limitation of human existence is expressed in four dimensions:

- *Logical limitations*: There are certain things we can't do simply because they can't be done. This is due not to human weakness but to the unbending nature of reality. You can't make, design, or even conceive of a square circle; it's a logical impossibility. You can't write a five-line Elizabethan sonnet. These limitations apply to any inherently contradictory situation.
- *Physical limitations*: We can do many things, but always within the potential of our nature. You and I can't fly out of our window, choose to live to a ripe old age of 529, or grow taller or shorter at will. Our body and our control over physical matter are subject to some very real limitations.
- *Intellectual limitations*: No human person is omniscient. For every piece of data we know there is an infinite amount of information of which we are ignorant. As a

philosopher said, "The more I know, the more I realize how little I know." Our understanding of things is never complete.

- *Moral limitations*: In a *proper* sense this limitation refers to our inability to always choose good, without a special supernatural grace. In a *secondary* sense, it means that we are subject to the moral law, and not above it. We are free to choose to *do* good or evil, but we can't *make* something good or evil simply by willing it. We are free to steal, but we can't convert theft into an act of virtue by sheer willpower. It will remain an evil act whether we recognize it or not. Right and wrong are not human inventions. Morality corresponds to objective good and evil which we are free to embrace or reject.

The presence of constraints is an indispensable condition for the exercise of freedom. I am free to play baseball as long as there are limits to my freedom, that is, provided there are rules that I must follow. If I can put an unlimited number of players on the field, say, 34, instead of nine, it spoils the game; I'm no longer free to play baseball. Changing the rules along the way would make the game ridiculous.

Freedom without constraints is like a body with no bones or a company undecided as to whether its aim is to make money or to lose it. Everything becomes pointless when there is no structure, no clear objective or direction. Freedom needs limitations as a river needs its banks, or a rifle its barrel.

Freedom and Self-control

Freedom is found not in blindly following our impulses, but in self-mastery. We may believe we are free while in reality we are slaves to things: our appetites, our passions, public opinion, fashions, peer-pressure, and so forth. St. Peter, when writing to the early Church, pointed out the contradiction of those who proclaim liberty by abandoning themselves to their bodily desires: "They may promise freedom, but they themselves are slaves, slaves to corruption; because if anyone lets himself be dominated by anything, then he is a slave to it" (2 Peter 2:19). Slavery of the body is just one kind of bondage; slavery of the will is worse.

Freedom is like being in shape. Anyone is free to climb Mt. Everest, but many are unable to do so because they are out of shape. There are no external restrictions but there is an internal one. As we have said, freedom is more than wanting, it is the power to bring about what we want. If I want to quit smoking but cannot because of my lack of willpower, I am not free. My will is out of shape.

Human freedom is freedom of the whole

person, not freedom of a particular part. For a spouse to be free to be faithful, he must have control of his passions. Without this self-control, there is no freedom. Imagine the case of a race car driver. He is free to drive only if he has total control over his vehicle. He has to be able to stop, to accelerate, to turn at a moment's notice. These maneuvers demand strict control over these different parts and are necessary to be free to drive.

If I am going skiing, I sharpen the edges of my skis. They are no longer free to slip back and forth, but now I am free to turn and to stop. Control of the parts under a common direction is necessary for freedom of the whole.

We are free not because there is nothing holding us back but because, with God's grace, we are able to pursue our true end and destiny as children of God. If freedom were simply letting loose and following our base passions and instincts, then animals would be freer than humans. They are uninhibited by reason or conscience. Instinct and reflex is their law.

True freedom is the ability to direct our feelings, passions, tendencies, emotions, desires, and fears under the government of reason and will. Thus understood, freedom requires that individuals truly be master of themselves, determined to fight and overcome the different forms of selfishness and individualism which threaten their maturity as persons. Truly free persons are open to others, generous in dedication and service to their neighbor.

THE TRUTH WILL SET YOU FREE

Jesus Christ, when standing trial for blasphemy and for opposing the payment of taxes to Caesar, was made to appear before the Roman procurator, Pontius Pilate. Pilate questioned Jesus about His teaching and Jesus replied, "I have come to bear witness to the truth. Anyone committed to the truth hears My voice." And the procurator, who could easily be a spokesman for our modern world, scoffed and retorted, "Truth? What is that?"

Some people today are not awfully interested in the truth, though they pay it lip-service. To many it matters more how they feel towards a particular idea, and how it affects them, than whether or not it corresponds to objective truth. This is very comfortable, of course. You believe what you want to believe, I believe what I want, and we'll all be happy together. This is pluralism, right? This is "respect" for one another. We all have our own ideas — on religion, politics, abortion, and marriage, and that's okay.

Let's take an example. Frank loves carrots. For Stephanie carrots are nothing to write home about, but she's a big fan of corn on the cob. Now why should Stephanie waste her breath extolling the glories and salutary benefits of corn on the cob if Frank is perfectly content with his carrots? In short, what right do you have to impose your way of thinking on someone else?

That's all very well and good if we're talking about culinary preferences. I have no right to impose my views, because they are simply my views, my preferences, my taste. But truth is not like vegetables. The truth is more than just my way of looking at things; the truth is the way things are in themselves. And fact is not just what is demonstrable by mathematical proof, but what *is*. The truth imposes itself and demands to be heard.

In a sense it could be argued that knowledge makes us less free. Once I find out that the moon is a small, lifeless planet I am no longer free to believe that it is a silver disk, or a circular cross-section of green cheese. The more I know, the less I am free to think whatever I want. If you have a hard time accepting this, try believing that $2 + 2$ equals 256. No strength of will can convince your mind that $2 + 2$ equals anything other than 4. That is because our intelligence is not a free faculty. It always seeks the truth.

Usually this isn't too tough for us because our knowledge doesn't impinge on our lifestyle. But if a certain truth will make me change my personal practices, I may be reluctant to accept it for fear it should cramp my style. That's why there's very little debate among Christians concerning the nature of the Blessed Trinity, while the Church's teaching on abortion and contraception is a perpetual battleground. Not that the mystery of the Blessed Trinity is somehow easier to understand than sexual ethics. Far from it. But where a person's lifestyle is concerned, it is much harder to seek the truth with objectivity.

The great Italian writer Alessandro Manzoni once wrote that if the acceptance of mathematical truths had practical moral consequences, we would see major debates over the validity of the Pythagorean theorem. That is why Christ said, "Anyone committed to the *truth* hears My voice." The problem is that at times we are more committed to our personal *preferences* than to the *truth*.

Yet in another, more real and important way, knowledge — that is, the truth — makes me freer. My knowledge frees me from doubt, ignorance and error, and empowers me to make better decisions. To be truly free, we must cultivate an unconditional devotion to the truth.

Freedom and Christianity

We have often heard the accusation leveled against Christianity that it seeks to reduce our freedom. Nonetheless Christ claimed to be the Truth, and promised that the Truth would set us free. Is Christianity the great defender of human freedom or its oppressor?

If we truly want to do what is right, we first must know the difference between right and wrong. This is a first condition for our freedom. Secondly, not only must we be able to distinguish what is right, we must also have the strength to carry it out. Christianity promises both these elements: (1) enlightenment to know right from wrong and (2) God's grace, the strength to carry it out.

Christianity reveals God to us in the Person of Jesus Christ. Christ taught and showed us by His own example the difference between right and wrong, good and evil, how to please God and the things that displease Him. The Church carries on Christ's mission as He commanded her: "Go, therefore and teach all nations. . ."

Many today would insist that by teaching us to discern between right and wrong, the Church is curtailing our freedom. In reality, the opposite is true. In teaching us to discern between right and wrong, the Church is clarifying our alternatives so that we can make an *informed* decision. How can I be free to choose what I don't know? The Church as teacher enlightens us and permits us to decide with a clear head between right and wrong. Moral ignorance confuses the two, which makes the choice very difficult, and thus limits our freedom.

Jesus declared that He is the light of the world. Light allows us to see, to know the truth of our surroundings, to walk with confidence and to understand where we are going. Darkness is not freedom. Those who would say that Christianity is a limitation of freedom are those who would rather live in the dark; they prefer the enslavement of ignorance to the freedom of the truth.

A Christian is truly, genuinely free, especially for three reasons, two of which we have already seen: through the *knowledge* of God's will, the *strength* of God's grace, and the unmerited *gift* of salvation. That is why St. Paul identifies Christianity with freedom. In Christ we find the fullness of humanity, the blueprint and model of what it means to be fully human. In Him we experience the truth of our existence and destiny, and moreover receive the strength to live according to that truth.

THE GREATEST TRIUMPH

Freedom is the root of our dignity as human beings. That is to say, dignity begins with freedom but doesn't end there. A root is not a whole tree, nor is freedom the ultimate goal of human existence. Freedom provides the possibility for our greatest triumph as creatures made in God's image: *love*, the pouring out of oneself for another. Love is impossible without freedom. In fact, many human beings — essentially free — are not as yet capable of love, because love requires a higher freedom, the power to forget yourself, to put someone else ahead of you, and many are unable to do that. The greatest human acts demand the greatest degree of freedom. Human liberty in its fullest and deepest meaning is the principal driving force for the responsible giving of oneself to another. That is the true use of freedom and its most profound expression. The sincere gift of self is the privileged path to authentic personal fulfillment.

Love is the highest form of freedom. "Love, and do as you please," was St. Augustine's startling maxim. Love sums up all that is good. It seeks the good of the other but ends up furnishing the greatest possible good to the one who loves. This is no surprise, since, as St. John reminds us, "God is love, and he who lives in love, lives in God" (1 Jn 4:16).

CULTIVATING PERSONAL FREEDOM

Throughout this chapter we have offered guidelines and tips to help us live in true liberty. Let us sum them up here in these four basic principles:

1. *Free persons are masters of themselves.* Those who allow themselves to be dominated by anything whatsoever are slaves to that thing. Freedom is found, not in giving in to

our impulses but in self-mastery. And this, of course, means self-discipline. This isn't always a pleasant or well-received recommendation, but if we are honest with ourselves we recognize its validity. Any athlete appreciates the value and necessity of sacrifice. If we are truly to be free, we must embrace sacrifice with courage and confidence.

2. *Free persons are devoted to the truth.* Truth is freedom from ignorance and doubt. To live as authentic human persons we must seek out, venerate, and live according to the truth: the meaning of life, the purpose of the things around us, the truth of our own being.

3. *Free persons exercise their freedom.* We grow in freedom when we exercise our liberty consciously, decidedly, and deliberately. When we allow routine to slip in, we become like a train car on a railroad track: pushed from behind, pulled from ahead, held in place by two iron rails. It is better to first establish where we are going, why, and how we are to get there. Then we can put all we are into our decisions and the living out of our commitments.

4. *Free persons think for themselves.* We must avoid being governed by public opinion, by what other people are doing, by ideas

and fads that are here today and gone tomorrow. We should stick to what we know is right, unafraid to call things by their name even at the risk of losing popularity or seeming to be out of step with the times.

As we have seen, freedom is much more than a catchy slogan invoked to justify our actions. It is a gift that requires careful administration if we are to use it well. In the next chapter we will examine the practical use of our freedom in making choices. It is there that our values make their impact on the course of our lives.

CHAPTER 4

VALUES IN ACTION:
MAKING CHOICES

Choice is the fabric of human life. From dawn to dusk our life is an unbroken chain of one choice after another. When you get up in the morning and put on your grey and maroon argyle socks instead of your white athletic socks, you have made a choice. As you get into bed in the evening and pull the covers up under your chin you may choose to read for a few minutes, watch television or, after having said your prayers, head right off to the land of Nod. All day long we are continually deciding what we're going to do, how we're going to do it, when we're going to do it, if we're going to keep doing it, and how long we're going to do it.

There are two ways of looking at this string of decision-making events, just as there are two ways of looking at life: we can imagine everything to be a succession of disconnected sensations and experiences, or we can regard life as a meaningful whole, a story or a journey. The first way of seeing things is an "MTV life-vision." The goblet of life's nectar is to be savored, relished, drained to the dregs. Live for the moment. According to this outlook, life is a series of vignettes, and choices are open-ended, free, and of little consequence. The most important thing is to be "true to your feelings."

From the second perspective, life is a voyage and you are the captain of the ship. Your choices are turns of the ship's wheel, which have a real effect on your journey. Or life is a story and you are the main character. You are the co-author of the story of your life, an adventure with an involved, fascinating plot that unfolds before your eyes as you live it. Your past, present and future are parts of an uninterrupted and meaningful continuum.

Choices are the reflection of values, just as values are the backdrop against which all our choices are made. That is to say, our values are the driving force behind our individual choices. If you value order, this is reflected in your choice to keep your clothes well arranged in your closet, in your decision to organize the things on your desk before sitting down to work, etc. Choice and values are inseparable companions. Our individual decisions are the concrete manifestations of our values.

WHAT'S IN A CHOICE?

Not all choices have the same impact on our lives. Some, like marriage, mark a new beginning or a major shift in lifestyle. Others, like the choice of the necktie you put on in the morning, have little bearing on the rest of your life. Yet all choices, small or great, share certain essential elements that can be reduced to five: (1) freedom to choose, (2) alternatives, (3) deliberation, (4) renunciation, and (5) the act of choosing. Each ingredient is necessary and where even one is missing there is no choice.

Freedom to Choose

Choice is grounded on a basic premise: human freedom. Simply put, where there is no freedom there can be no choice. Although there are those who deny free will, our personal experience and common sense assure us that human freedom is a reality. You and I are free to act as we please.

Freedom to choose depends on consciousness, reflection and willpower. It is not a blind reaction to a stimulus, the way an animal responds instinctively, but the capacity of deciding after having reflected on the possibilities. When this capacity is exercised, we engage in active decision-making.

Passivity, on the other hand, is choosing not to exercise our freedom. It is allowing other people and events to make our choices for us. Passivity is like getting on a train to see where it takes us, or floating in the middle of a river, letting the current carry us where it will. It is the abdication of our right and our duty to be the protagonist of our own destiny.

Yet we are obliged to choose. Life is made up of constant decisions, one after another, and because of our nature as free beings we can't get around the necessity of making choices. Passivity says, "I don't want to choose." But in reality even if we decide not to choose, we still have made a choice. If every day Bill goes to ask Susie, "Will you marry me?" and every day Susie replies, "I don't know; ask me again tomorrow," at the end of her life Susie is still unmarried and in fact she *has* made that choice.

Choices are not disconnected. Since life is a story, your big decisions deeply affect the less significant daily choices you face. In fact, these lesser choices often stem directly from your basic decisions as many branches spring from a common trunk or many roads originate from a common avenue. Every choice is a fork in the road.

If you're driving along a side street in Pennsylvania and decide to get on Interstate 80, the new alternatives that present themselves will all be determined by that choice. You would have never encountered the next exits you come upon if you had not taken I-80. Likewise there are many alternatives you will never consider because you didn't select the roads that lead to them.

In the poem, "The Road Not Taken," Robert Frost beautifully portrays this image and illustrates the importance and transcendence of life's decisions:

Two roads diverged in a yellow wood,
And sorry I could not travel both
And be one traveler, long I stood. . .

Our present choices determine our future alternatives. Once we have set out on a certain path, the crossroads we come upon will be those that meet up with that particular road.

Consider the case of the children's tale *Peter Pan*. Peter, the immortal elfling, falls in love with the little girl Wendy, an ordinary person. He is offered the choice of remaining as he is without her or becoming an ordinary person with her. This was the fork in his road. And as Chesterton so keenly put it, "Even in fairyland you cannot walk down two roads at once." There is only one choice to be made.

Although your present choices affect your future alternatives, they don't hamper or diminish your essential human freedom. If you are faithful to your commitments and true to your word, it is not because your freedom is conditioned by the decision you have made. It is because you freely ratify and confirm today the choice you made yesterday.

Alternatives

Some evening at about 6:30 your rumbling stomach lets you know it's time to eat. You go to the refrigerator and find it bare. You next open up the cupboard and sitting off by itself in the corner is a can of warm-and-serve *Chef Boyardee* mini ravioli. In this case you clearly have no choice as to your dinner menu. It's ravioli or starve (of course starvation is also an option, but we'll disregard it). We can only make a choice when we are presented with at least two alternatives.

If you send out applications to sixteen different universities and are accepted for admission to just one, no decision need be made because there are simply no alternatives.

In order for there to be a choice not only must there be at least two alternatives, but you must be *aware* of the alternatives. It wouldn't be any help in the above example to find out the next morning that besides the can of mini ravioli in the cupboard there was also a closet full of groceries where you didn't even think of looking. They were there but you didn't know it; so as far as your decision is concerned, it is as if they never existed at all. Or if after you had applied to sixteen colleges your little brother, unbeknownst to you, was systematically opening up your acceptance letters and making paper airplanes out of them, they wouldn't do you much good because you can't choose what you don't know.

Deliberation

The intellectual aspect of decision-making is called deliberation. It is a thoughtful weighing of the possibilities according to the pluses and minuses of each one. "This Chrysler is nicer looking and has air-conditioning. The Chevy was less expensive and gets better gas mileage. . ." There are many things to be taken into account to make a good decision.

Not all choices demand the same amount of deliberation. Often we run on that particularly convenient auto-pilot called "habit." There are many different knots that *could* be employed to secure one's shoes, but it is rare that we ever depart from the standard bow knot we learned as kids. We tie it in a flash, without thinking. Imagine if you had to ponder every tug of the lace, every over and under, each time you put on your shoes!

Shoe-tying is just one example. A golf neophyte has his head full of a hundred and one directives as he sidles up to the ball nestled in the grass: legs apart, head down, pull from the shoulder, shift weight, body pivot, wrist snap, etc. With so many counsels to keep in mind, he's lucky if he hits the ball. But after hundreds of hours at the driving range, many of these directives become superfluous. The golf stroke becomes second nature.

We are creatures of habit, and perhaps this is what keeps us from going crazy. If we had to think through every little step of driving a car, speaking, walking, eating, and dressing, we would be mentally drained by the ten o'clock coffee break.

The formation of habits frees up the mind for

more important choices. Instead of deliberating over which finger forms the loop in a bow knot, you're busy thinking about a business engagement or the presentation you are to give in the afternoon. Instead of concentrating on keeping your left arm straight, you're considering exactly where you want the ball to drop on the green. Instead of consciously putting one foot in front of the other, you're thinking of where you want to go.

Renunciation

The fourth element of every choice is the aspect of *renunciation*. This may come as a surprise to us because we're accustomed to viewing choice not as a denial of something, but rather as an exercise of our liberty to do something. But this is just one side of the coin. The word decision comes from the Latin *de-cidere*, which means "to cut away." Selecting a part always implies leaving aside the rest.

Do you remember when you were little and your Mom would take you to the ice cream parlor? She would ask you what flavor you wanted, and after some moments of painful indecision, you would say, Daiquiri Ice or Chocolate Marble or Rum Raisin. And why was that choice so tough to make? Why are decisions at times still so difficult? Because the minute you said Rum Raisin you eliminated Cookies & Cream, Blue Moon, Chunky

Monkey, and all the other wonderful possibilities tugging at your taste buds. Because of our limited capacity every choice is a renunciation. We would love to choose everything, "They all look so good!"

In the same way, we only have one life to live and our choices take on a special weight because of that limitation. We should make our choices with realism and reflection, aware of what they imply. If we had many lives, we could try everything and still not exhaust our possibilities. As it stands, we have one shot at life so we had better get it right the first time.

The Act of Choosing

But these first four elements of choice still don't tell the whole story. They only bring us to the brink of the decision. The stage is set, everything is in place, but one final component is necessary: the choice itself, the act of choosing. This may seem rather evident, but it is the essence of choice, when *what could be* passes into *what is*. The other four components are merely the necessary conditions for choice to be possible.

There are two types of choices: intellectual decisions and lived choices. It is not the same to decide to do something as to do it. One thing is the plan, the other is the execution, and both are a type of choice. As Shakespeare reminds us, "If *to do* were as easy as *to know what were good to do*, chapels had been churches, and poor men's cottages princes' palaces." In other words, choice is not only an act of the intelligence, but also an act of the will.

Consider the small boy at the swimming pool who decided it was high time he dived off the three-meter board like the older children. He marched resolutely up the steps, took one look at the water below, and marched resolutely down. Or again, how many have decided to follow a strict diet, selected their regimen and then fallen miserably at the first offer of assorted munchies or strawberry cheesecake? When push comes to shove, our choices become real in our actions.

Today there is a widespread attitude of fear in the face of decisions, which can only be termed a mentality of non-commitment. Many lack the fundamental maturity needed to commit themselves to a project, to an ideal, to a person — especially when the commitment is for life. Where does this attitude come from? As we have seen, commitment — that is, the exercise of freedom — is seen as limiting personal liberty. As soon as I commit myself, I'm in a bind. I have eliminated my other possibilities and I'm stuck with the aftermath of the choice I've made.

Every choice is total in the sense that the past is irrevocable: I can never go back and repeat what I have or haven't done. Yet I find my happiness and personal fulfillment precisely *here*: in the responsible exercise of my freedom, and not in amassing a great store of potential freedom never to be put to use.

A rich man who never spends any money out of fear of becoming poor ends up living as a pauper (the very result he was trying to avoid). The mentality of non-commitment poses a similar paradox. Those who are afraid to commit their life to a cause, an ideal or a person, live as if they had no freedom at all, for fear that should they commit themselves they would lose what freedom they have.

In every choice, especially the basic choices in life, you accept a certain degree of incertitude. How will you feel five years from now? How do you know that so-and-so won't change? How can you be absolutely sure it's your vocation? The beauty of fidelity is precisely this —that a mature individual commits himself or herself without knowing all the consequences of their pledge. The faithful person proves his or her worth by hanging tough even in trying times.

THE BIG FOUR

Having considered the components of choice, we can turn our attention to different types of decisions. Choices can be classified by their degree of transcendence. To "transcend" is to go beyond the moment. Transcendent choices are those that most profoundly affect our lives and those of others. Some choices have little influence on life; others are radical and condition the rest of our decisions.

The day Caesar chose to cross the Rubicon, he also made many other decisions which have long since been forgotten. Every day we make many choices; some are trifling, others produce ripples in the four corners of our existence.

The two qualities that determine the transcendence of a choice are its *depth* and its *permanence*. Depth refers to the involvement of the person in the choice. The choice to move to Oregon and join a commune would certainly affect me more deeply than the decision to order a Big Mac instead of a Quarter Pounder with Cheese. More of my *person* would be committed.

Permanence is the time-factor of our decisions. A choice whose effects can be felt for a long time is clearly more transcendent than one that passes like a shooting star. The decision to get tattooed is more transcendent than putting on make-up in the morning that will be washed off in the evening.

We make very few earth-shaking decisions in life. Most of our days are spent living out the consequences of choices we've made. Then again, we don't always recognize the transcendence of our decisions at the moment we make them.

It was in a sense a historic moment when Mrs. Jordan decided to give her son Michael a basketball for his birthday instead of a ukelele or a subscription to *Bird Watchers' Weekly*. The day Johann and Maria Beethoven decided to sign up young Ludwig for piano classes (instead of sending him for swimming lessons or enrolling him in architecture school) was truly a momentous hour both for Beethoven and for music. Sometimes the consequences of our decisions only surface with time.

While some decisions turn out to be significant because of the way things unfold, others are weighty by nature. These deserve more reflection and forethought. It will be worthwhile to take a moment to consider the four most important choices people normally face in life.

Choice of a Career

One big decision which most people make is the choice of a career. This is the least transcendent of the four categories we will examine, and it varies for different individuals. For some people, a career is simply the most convenient means to put bread on the table and keep the gas tank full. An ever growing number of people change careers one or more times during their adult life as new opportunities open up.

For others, especially where years of education and training are involved, the decision takes on greater significance. A doctor, for example, invests many years in preparation. The motivation for this choice often comes from the desire to do something worthwhile with one's life and to make a real contribution to the good of society.

Choice of a Vocation

A second major decision is the choice of a vocation. Vocation here doesn't refer to a trade we learn as an apprentice, or a course of study to be pursued in college. That is why vocation doesn't fall under the same heading as career. Vocation has its own specific characteristics.

A vocation (Latin: *vocare*, to call) is a calling, a particular path of service of God and our fellow men. It is the lifestyle God has marked out for each person, the mission He created each one for. Traditionally Christians have recognized three distinct vocations: (1) marriage, (2) the single life, (3) the consecrated life (i.e. belonging exclusively to God) which includes the priesthood, religious life, and consecrated lay life.

Unfortunately the notion of vocation has also suffered much distortion over the last thirty years, and many young people today never even think to question what God may be asking of them in life. But it is one of the most serious questions we face. If God made me, He knows what He made me for. It is true that He made me to be *happy*, but who really knows better what will make me happy in the long run — He or I? It isn't difficult to lose track of the elementary truth of our lives: where we come from, where we are going, and how to get there.

It's important for young people to consider this question objectively, prayerfully, and generously. Is God calling me to be a priest, a religious, a married person, a consecrated lay person? This isn't something to be taken for granted. A common response to this question is: "I just want to be normal, to do what most people do." But people aren't mass-produced like automobiles or computers. God made me personally, loves me personally, and created me for a purpose. He didn't make me to just be "normal" or "one of the crowd."

Choice of a Spouse

A third basic choice the majority of individuals face is the choice of a husband or wife. The depth, the beauty and the importance of this step must not be underestimated, especially in an era when this fundamental human institution has suffered such violence and distortion.

It is disconcerting to witness the superficial approach many people take towards marriage as opposed to other, far less important decisions. Think, for instance, of buying a car. Many spend months researching different makes and models, consulting experts and car owners, asking questions about everything from gas mileage to warranties, from electrical systems to tire durability. Everything has to be just right. Why? Because the car is an investment; it has to last four or five years.

Yet any mere purchase is infinitely more trivial than the choice of a spouse, your lifelong companion, partner and best friend. A husband and wife are embarking on one of the greatest adventures life has to offer: the forming of a family, a home, the fundamental building block of society itself.

Society's shallow attitude toward marriage is mirrored in the considerations taken into account when deciding to get married. Often the deepest issues are skipped over and frivolous reasons receive the most attention. The most important element of compatibility between a man and woman is not that they like to play backgammon together, or that they have any other hobby or pastime in common, nor that they find each other attractive.

These secondary aspects have their place, but the most vital ingredient of their life together is that they share a common life-vision, faith, ideals and goals for their future family. When there is unity in what is most basic and essential, there can be give and take in other, less important aspects. But when life-ideals, beliefs and aspirations don't coincide, grave problems are bound to emerge when the honeymoon gives way to the reality of life together.

Choice to Live as a Christian

A fourth vital choice faced by believers is the decision to be — or not to be — a Christian. Notice this isn't the same as the choice to merely bear the name Christian, like a framed certificate on the wall, nor even of carrying the mark of baptism on your soul (your initiation into the Church and the starting gate of your Christian life). Running a race is far more than that initial burst launching you from the starting block. It is a progression: a journey from one point to another.

The decision to be a Christian is the choice to be a follower of Jesus Christ, to accept the salvation He offers and to commit yourself to live according to His teachings. Belief and action combine to form the essence of Christianity. Our choice stems from the conviction that Jesus Christ is the Son of God, that He came to earth, lived and died to save us, and rose from the dead as proof of His victory over death. But it also implies a certain lifestyle. Christianity is not intellectual belief divorced from practical living. It is a way of life in accord with the example and teachings of the One Whose name it bears: Jesus Christ.

If we were to ask Christ Himself about the most important decisions in life, what would He tell us?

For Christ the most basic human option boils down to the choice between life and death. As we mentioned in the first chapter, our Lord's words are simple and clear: "What does it profit a man if he gains the whole world and loses his soul? What can a man offer in exchange for his soul?" (Mt 16:26). This is the main choice life offers us: the path of eternal life and the road leading to eternal death. This is hard to swallow, because it has a definitive tone. But they are Christ's own words. The various choices we make now — big and little — form part of the one, radical choice between life and death.

Christ speaks of a division of all people on the day of judgment according to their choice to either live for others or to live for themselves. He compares it to a shepherd separating sheep from goats, each group with its distinct destination. He says to those on his right (the sheep), "Come blessed of My Father, inherit the Kingdom prepared for you. For I was hungry and you gave Me to eat, I was thirsty and you gave Me to drink, naked and you clothed Me, sick and in prison and you visited Me" (Mt 25:34-36).

They respond, saying that they had never seen Him in any of those conditions, but He replies, "As often as you did it (or neglected to do it) to one of these least brothers of Mine, you did it (or neglected to do it) to Me" (Mt 25:40). Christianity goes to the heart of life, affecting all our decisions. A Christian is truly a new person.

Clearly the choice to live as a Christian doesn't

mean the struggle is over. It's not a one-time decision. By choosing to live as true Christians we aren't suddenly freed from temptation or difficulties, but it does give our lives a basic orientation.

FUNDAMENTAL OPTION

Of all choices we make, there is one that sets the horizons and the framework of life. It is within this *fundamental option* that all other decisions are made. Implicitly or explicitly we give our life a basic direction, a comprehensive meaning.

Man's life is a unity. Running through all our actions and decisions is a common thread. For each person there exists a principle, a profound life-orientation, a life-ideal, that the person aspires to fulfill, and to which all other values or projects are subordinated. The fundamental life option is not a particular act which precedes other particular acts. It is an underlying attitude and elemental orientation that is tacitly present in all our choices.

The word "option" is intentionally used rather than "choice," because its meaning is broader and deeper than choice. It doesn't aim at a particular objective but embraces the whole of existence. This option determines the meaning intended to be conferred on one's life and the orientation impressed upon one's actions.

Saying that it is *fundamental* emphasizes the fact that it touches the core and ultimate foundations of human existence, the relationship of a person with himself and with God. It expresses a dilemma between two opposing possibilities, which, according to St. Thomas Aquinas, boils down to a choice for or against God. It forms the groundwork for all future choices.

The human person is ordered to an ultimate purpose, not just to *particular* "goods." In every act we perform, we make ourselves who we are as a person. We choose our end by choosing the means. If a person says, "I want such and such," but his actions do not lead to that end, we can only conclude that he really doesn't want it, or at least there is something else he wants more.

Our choices are both an expression of self and a producing of self. Every choice *reveals* our true inner person and our fundamental option and, at the same time makes us what we are. Babe Ruth was a great baseball player who hit many home-runs. Or better, each time he got a home-run he was *making himself* into a great baseball player. We would never think of calling him a great baseball player if he never got a hit. In the same way, our small decisions are an *expression* of the orientation of our life but also *define* that orientation.

If you choose to tell a lie, you have opted not only for that isolated *act*; you have also opted *to be* the type of person who would tell a lie. There is no such thing as an honest person who does dishonest things. One who habitually does dishonest things is a dishonest person.

As Christ said, "Can people pick grapes from thorns, or figs from thistles? In the same way, a sound tree produces good fruit but a rotten tree bad fruit. A sound tree cannot bear bad fruit, nor a rotten tree bear good fruit. . . you will know them by their fruits" (Mt 7:16-20). Our actions are a manifestation of who we are. Our lifestyle — the sum total of our actions and attitudes — is the clearest external expression of our fundamental life option.

Turnarounds of 180 degrees are rare in life. More often we change little by little, imperceptibly. Judas wasn't born a traitor and Teresa of Avila wasn't born a saint. A generous person may gradually, subtly, in the smallest things begin to become less generous. A selfish individual can also grow better, by choosing to do what is kind and good more and more in the countless opportunities of every day. In every free act our fundamental life option is either ratified, modified, or revised.

SOLID DECISIONS

We have spoken about choices, their components, and the different types of vital decisions life confronts us with. But there remains the most practical issue: how can I *make* good decisions? How can I *reach* the level of maturity where I am truly free, able to commit myself without fear, and live out my commitments with serenity and joy? We will consider five stable principles to serve as guidelines for making mature, prudent choices throughout life.

1. *Know what you want.* If you still aren't sure what you want in life, if you haven't reached the point where you can say, "This is truly the meaning of life," it will be tough to make other choices. We won't know if they will bring us nearer to or further from our goal if we haven't yet established what our goal is. First things first. Decisions require principles. Chesterton conveyed something similar when he said, "The key to every problem is a principle, as the key to every cipher is a code. When a man knows his own principle of action he can act."

Many people take principles for granted and bury themselves in activities, without stopping to think about the meaning of these activities. We can lose the best years of our lives by basing our work on a series of illusions, emotions and impressions, instead of clear values and objectives. It's *worth* investing time and energy to search out the meaning of life. It is the most important question we can ask.

2. *Make your decisions based on what you will value in the long run, and not on the impressions or*

feelings of the moment. Dr. Spencer Johnson, in his best-seller *"Yes" or "No": A Guide to Better Decisions*, offers this simple tip to make better decisions: "To see what is really needed, I ask, 'What would I like to *have done?*'"

The familiar adage tells us that hindsight is 20/20; that is, looking back on our actions it is easy to judge whether we have decided well. We could try this experiment with the fundamental orientation of our life. We could project ourselves into the future to the very end of our lives. There, from that vantage point, we have a much clearer and more objective view of our lives. What does this "hindsight" tell us?

Many things which at the time seemed very important will undoubtedly take on a very relative value — or even seem insignificant — in the light of eternity. Other aspects of our life which didn't interest us much at the time will suddenly appear more worthy of attention. Material possessions, fame, personal achievement and power over others will undoubtedly matter very little. Deeds of kindness, dedication and love will suddenly shine with a special splendor. What will bring us satisfaction at the end of our lives, at the threshold of passing on from this brief sojourn on the earth? A life well lived will be our greatest consolation.

3. *Reflect well before choosing.* Deliberation should be proportional to the transcendence of the decision. There are those who impulsively dive

right into commitments which they later regret. Others follow their feelings instead of their reason. Still others are irresolute and have a hard time making even the most simple decisions. We mustn't be afraid to finally make the choice, to commit ourselves to an ideal or a way of life. There will never be 100% certainty. We must learn to be prudent in making choices, and decisive and energetic in carrying them out.

The process of deliberation often includes consulting others. It is helpful to seek the guidance of wise people whose lives bear witness to the solidity of their own principles and decisions. A good friend who can help us discern the proper course to follow in the midst of doubt and indecision is a true treasure.

4. *Renew your key decisions every day.* Never let them become routine or take them for granted. Your vital decisions touch what is deepest in your soul. They are acts of love, acts of deep commitment of your person. Something this profound shouldn't be passed over lightly or allowed to grow stale. Every day we must recommit ourselves, freely confirm the choices we have made, especially when faithfulness to our commitments is difficult and requires sacrifice.

Renew your ideal. Keep it before you always and never let it fade from view. Renew your love for your vocation, that unique path and state in life God chose for you with immeasurable, personal love. Renew your love for God, your love for Jesus Christ. This love is expressed in your commitment to follow Him through thick and thin, to be true to His will for you, true to His Church, true to His commandments, especially the commandment of love.

These options you have made are the real foundation of your life, the things which give sense and meaning to your work, sweat, efforts and tears.

"Renewing" isn't the same as questioning the commitments you have made, or reconsidering your decisions over and over again. Renewing is "to make new again, to revitalize, to refresh." Renewal is the opposite of routine, that cancer of the soul which dries up life, leaving it withered and faded, like a flower without fragrance or beauty. Renewal is the vitality of beginning again.

5. *Keep your eye on your destination.* To run a race well it's not enough to run hard and fast, to keep up a constant pace and not to give out. You must arrive at your destination. If you run hard and fast —but in the wrong direction, or make a wrong turn along the way — you not only won't win but will no longer even be in the race. To make good decisions you must know where you are going, and what you are after.

A basic rule of thumb is that if you don't know where you're going, you're never going to get there. Before stepping into the car and turning out of the driveway, it is helpful to know where you intend to go. It's true that you could just go out for a joyride with no particular destination in mind. But all roads lead somewhere. You will eventually arrive some place, and it might not be the sort of spot you had in mind. A wiser course of action is to identify your destination *first* and then plot out the route that will take you there.

Knowing where I'm going is certainly more than half the battle. It is worth little, however, unless I use this knowledge to actually reach my destination. Knowing how to get there means employing the appropriate measures to achieve my objective. There are many pleasant roads in the world, but only a certain combination will take me where I want to go. Boston Post Road is lovely, but if I am headed to Chicago it won't be much help to me.

With these principles in mind we will now turn our focus to those values that most affect us as persons. Of all the different types of choices we make, our *moral choices* carry a particular importance. They determine what kind of persons we are in a way that no other choices do. These moral or ethical choices are guided by our deepest values and will be the subject of our next chapter.

CHAPTER 5

MORAL VALUE

Hitler said it was an invention of the Jews. Freudians reduce it to the unconscious superego, and adherents of Transactional Analysis explain it away as the internalization of the parental role in a person. For something that purportedly doesn't exist, the conscience certainly gets more than its share of attention. For most of us the existence of conscience is an evident fact, borne out by daily personal experience, and is as obvious a reality as our mind, heart, teeth and fingernails.

Wrestling with conscience — precisely because it is inseparable from human experience — is one of the favorite perennial themes of literature. Poe's *Telltale Heart*, Hawthorne's *Scarlet Letter*, Shakespeare's *Macbeth* and Dostoyevsky's *Crime and Punishment* touch a chord at the heart of our being, and dramatize moral experiences each of us has lived first hand.

If life is made up of one choice after another, surely our moral choices are the most salient. The decisions of conscience are our moments for greatness. Perhaps this is part of the reason generation after generation finds a fascination with these literary works and considers them classics.

Despite our familiarity with conscience, it remains a nebulous notion we have trouble putting our finger on. What comes to mind when we hear the word "conscience"?

Perhaps the imagination conjures up a vision of two small figures perched on either shoulder, one all decked out in a white satin gown, golden wings and a shimmering halo; the second outfitted with trident, horns, red leotards and a nasty expression on his face. Or perhaps "conscience" calls to mind Pinocchio's companion Jimminy Cricket, exhorting the adventuresome marionette to "always let your conscience be your guide."

When a classroom of small children was asked what conscience is, one tyke responded that it is "a little bell that goes off when we do what we shouldn't."

All of these illustrations tell us something about conscience, but none offers us the complete picture.

RIGHT AND WRONG

Before moving on to conscience itself, we ought to first take a look at the concept of right and wrong. In 1980 when I was studying at the University of Michigan, one of my fellow students in a psychology course had a hard time accepting a particular mode of behavior advocated by the professor. He raised his hand and asked, "But is that *right*?" After a moment of silence the professor answered, "I prefer not to use the terms 'right' and 'wrong'; for me, everything is better described as either 'practical' or 'impractical'." My companion accepted that response, though the expression on his face revealed that he was somewhat disconcerted by the notion that all morality could be boiled down to simple pragmatism.

Our experience of moral obligation is altogether unique, substantially different from every other human experience. We encounter it at the core of our identity as free, responsible human persons. In his book, *The Problem of Pain*, C.S. Lewis masterfully expresses the singularity of this phenomenon:

> All the human beings that history has heard of acknowledge some kind of morality; that is, they feel towards certain proposed actions the experiences expressed by the words "I ought" or "I ought not." These experiences [. . .] cannot be logically deduced from the environment and physical experience of the man who undergoes them. You can shuffle "I want" and "I am forced" and "I shall be well advised" and "I dare not" as long

as you please without getting out of them the slightest hint of ought and ought not. [...] Attempts to resolve the moral experience into something else always presuppose the very thing they are trying to explain.

It is important to recognize the existence of objective right and wrong to appreciate the value of conscience. Conscience directs our actions to the pursuit of good — a good which really exists and attracts us. There is a tendency of the human soul that urges us with the force of a mandate to *do good and avoid evil*. It is, as Newman terms it, "the voice of God in the soul." This compelling interior inclination was not taught to us by anyone, nor did we assimilate it from our culture, nor is it a decision we made for ourselves. It comes as a standard feature for all human beings.

Good is more than what appeals to me, what I find to be pleasant or useful. Something is *good* when it is what it was *meant to be*, and something is good for me when it helps me to be what *I* am meant to be. "Goodness" is the perfection of nature and the fullness of being. A good meal is a meal that does what a meal is meant to do: it tastes good and it nourishes. A meal of two Hostess Twinkies and a strawberry milk shake is not a good meal, though it may gratify certain tastes, because it lacks the most essential quality of a meal: nourishment. A football game is good when it contains all the elements for which the game is played: competitiveness, athletic prowess, fair play, and excitement.

So what can be said about a good person? If we are told that Samantha is a good person, we cannot infer from this that she is a world-class hockey player, intelligent, stunningly attractive, or an accomplished hang-glider. What we *do* know is that she is unselfish, honest, loyal, generous and kind. In other words, we know that she is *morally good*. Her actions correspond to an objective standard of goodness.

Regardless of the abundance (or dearth) of other qualities and talents, moral goodness is always the weight that tips the balance, qualifying a person as good or bad. What if, for instance, we were to draw up a Human Values Report Card for Adolf Hitler? It might look something like this:

HITLER, Adolf	
Bravery	B+
Astuteness	A
Intelligence	A-
Willpower	A+
Moral value *	F
Value as a person	F

Despite Hitler's high marks in other areas, his final grade as a person is a reflection of his moral life. Moral value stands head and shoulders above all other values. When we do good we are behaving in accordance with the truth of our being, because we are made in the image and likeness of God, Who is good. Wrongdoing, on the other hand, is the *denial* of this truth of our being; it is moral falsehood. Conscience is the voice of truth and it does everything it can to keep us from living a lie. The pangs of conscience tell us when our actions are out of synch with the truth of our being.

THE REAL YOU

The human person is endowed with different faculties, different capabilities of body and spirit. We can distinguish between what is true and what is false through the use of our intelligence. We can likewise differentiate between various sounds, sights and smells — hot and cold, loud and quiet, bright and dim, sweet and salty — by the use of our external senses. But it is through conscience that we recognize good and evil.

St. Thomas Aquinas defines conscience as "the practical judgment of our reason which decides on the goodness or badness of our human actions." It is awareness of moral truth, the faculty which tells us what is to be done or not done from moment to moment. Conscience is a kind of inner voice that urges us, "Do this. . . Don't do that. . ."

Analyzing popular notions of conscience reveals something of its nature, but these notions have a basic flaw. Often conscience seems to be outside of us, a sort of Big Brother that sits waiting to accuse us when we violate the moral law. In reality conscience is not a cold, random, external law, but a reasonable law written on our hearts. It is our reason itself that judges our actions.

You are your conscience. The real you — the deep, spiritual, transcendent you — *that* is conscience. We all recognize the opposing tendencies in our fallen nature. Our spirit is drawn upward while our passions and instincts ("the flesh") drag us down. This interior struggle between the flesh and the spirit is described by St. Paul in his letter to the Church at Rome:

> I cannot understand my own behavior. I fail to carry out the things I want to do, and I find myself doing the very things I hate. When I act against my own will, that means I have a self that acknowledges that the Law is good, and so the thing behaving in that way is not my self but sin living in me.
> The fact is, I know nothing of good living in me — living, that is, in my unspiritual self — for though the will to do what is good is in me, the performance is not,

with the result that instead of doing the good things I want to do, I carry out the sinful things I do not want. [. . .]
In my *inmost self* I dearly love God's Law, but I can see that my body follows a different law that battles against the law which my reason dictates. This is what makes me a prisoner of that law of sin which lives inside my body (Rm 7:15-23).

It is clear that Paul identifies with his inner spiritual self; that is the *real* Paul. The same expression is used by the Psalmist when he says, "I bless the Lord, Who is my counsellor, and in the night my *inmost self* instructs me" (Ps 16:7). Our view of conscience depends on our perspective on ourselves. If we recognize two opposing tendencies, we have to take sides. We have to decide which one is the "real" me.

If I identify with my passions and instinctive tendencies, if I consider them to be the real me, then conscience and reason are a straitjacket that I must try to cast off. This is the Freudian approach perpetuated in classical psychoanalysis and in movements that glorify the primitive and instinctual. Jean Jacques Rousseau's theory of education also springs from this vision of man. For Rousseau, the more primal and more instinctual the better. Out with reason, in with raw feelings. From this angle conscience becomes a taboo, a "superego," a personification of social norms to be overcome.

If, on the other hand, I identify with my spirit, which aspires to truth and goodness, then passions are a force to be harnessed and not a master to be served. No horse likes to be bridled, nor does our flesh like to be subdued. It all hinges on whether we consider ourselves horse or driver.

From a Christian perspective, we need to become a "new" creation in the Lord, identified with the spirit and the works of the spirit. "The spirit gives life, the flesh has nothing to offer" (Jn 6:63). When we follow the flesh and act against our conscience, we act against our authentic selves. When we follow our conscience, we respond to our deepest aspirations which lead to fulfillment and happiness.

MORAL EYESIGHT

Although conscience is the true inner self, it is not purely subjective. In making a judgment, conscience evaluates according to a certain standard or principle, and this standard is moral truth. Conscience is personal, but objective. It is personal in the same way that seeing is personal. We all see the same thing, but we see it in our own way.

Ten persons with healthy eyes will recognize that the American flag is red, white and blue, and adorned with stars and stripes. If a fellow

comes along saying it is green, purple and char-
treuse and features giraffes and triangles, we would
immediately conclude our friend was suffering
from impaired vision (if not worse). Likewise,
moral truth is seen by our moral eyesight: conscience.

Since conscience is the principle of our judgment, it is essential that it be correct or we will see
everything in a distorted way. Christ put it very
clearly when He compared our conscience to our
eyes: "The lamp of the body is the eye. If your eye
is sound your whole body will be filled with light,
but if your eye is diseased your whole body will be
filled with darkness, and what a darkness it will
be!" (Lk 11:34).

If a person's cornea is deformed, he may see
things as taller and thinner than they actually are.
Without an operation or corrective lenses he will
never be able to judge distance, depth or form
correctly. Some experts suggest, for example, that
the elongated figures of El Greco's paintings are
due to a visual dysfunction rather than a revolutionary technique. The same can happen with our
conscience. If it becomes bent out of shape, we'll
judge our actions in a distorted way — things that
are wrong will seem (or feel) right, while things
that are right may appear wrong.

Today conscience is often glorified as a sort
of unerring guide of conduct, the single undispu-
table reference point for good and evil. "This is a

personal matter between me and my conscience." "You follow your conscience, I'll follow mine." "As long as it's okay according to your conscience it's all right."

This attitude stems from a moral subjectivism which holds that all things depend on one's point of view, and that there are no moral absolutes. What is right for one person has no relation to what is right or wrong for another. Through this subjectivism we could be led to feel morally justified to do whatever we please as long it conforms to our subjective conscience.

This subjectivism leads to a sort of "cafeteria morality," by which people select which doctrines, dogmas, moral norms and teachings appeal to them or coincide with their lifestyle. Yet even St. Paul, who strove to do good with all his might, confessed that conscience is not his ultimate judge — because it could be mistaken. "My conscience does not charge me with anything, but I am not for that reason acquitted. The Lord alone is my judge" (1 Cor 4:4).

We are not ourselves the ultimate foundation of moral value. We are gauged and measured by the objective order of right reason. In the case of human inventions *we* write rules for the game. But in the case of right and wrong there are fixed standards. The willful killing of an innocent person — to take an obvious example — is always morally wrong, and it is up to us to conform ourselves to this standard instead of conforming the standard to our opinions.

In the depths of our conscience we recognize the existence of a law we didn't write, but which we feel we must obey. We have the power to *do* right or wrong, but we do not have the power to *declare* what is right and wrong and have it be so. We can decide we don't need oxygen, but after a minute or so our body will remind us that it was not consulted in the decision. We could declare that cyanide is healthy, but if we take it we're buying a one-way ticket to the county morgue. Certain things are the way they are despite our opinions or personal wishes.

At the same time, right and wrong are not arbitrary but reasonable. They're not merely the whims of some capricious lawgiver. Fairness, for example, is good — really good. It is not a notion that struck God's fancy one day as He sat down to write the Ten Commandments. It is good because it is good. God doesn't command honesty, justice, temperance and religion because He *feels* like it, but because they are true "goods" for us. What is morally good is also unfailingly "good for us." In fact, the more we look into goodness, the more attractive and satisfying we realize it to be in every way.

Returning to our example of the ship, our conscience guides us in much the same way a compass helps a ship stay on course. A compass indicates North. From this we can ascertain what bearing the ship is following, and rectify our course according to our established route. If the compass is true, all the helmsman needs to do is follow the arrow North and he'll be sure of going North. If the compass is faulty, it may read North for what is actually Southeast. Instead of going to Nova Scotia, he may wind up in Cuba. That is, he will be "subjectively" correct but "objectively" in error.

More Than a Feeling

The judgment of conscience is an intellectual activity. It's an act of reason rather than a feeling. We usually feel good after doing what is right and feel bad after doing what is wrong, but conscience itself is not a feeling. Many activities produce feelings, but the activities themselves are not feelings. We may "feel good" playing baseball or attending a birthday party, but baseball and parties aren't feelings. We don't feel too good sitting in the dentist's chair, but a dentist's chair isn't a feeling either. A feeling is the *result* of something else — an effect. So feelings frequently *accompany* the activity of the conscience, but conscience isn't a feeling.

The judgments of conscience are not isolated flashes of moral insight, but reasoned conclusions. When you *feel* bad after lying to get out of a difficult situation, it's because your conscience is judging your action and in the light of objective principles, it tells you you've done wrong: "You should always tell the truth. It is wrong to lie. You have done wrong." In reality this process is often instantaneous and moral judgments become second nature, but they continue to be rational judgments. You don't just *feel* like you've done wrong — you *know* it.

This important distinction can save us from some common fallacies concerning feelings and morality. Sometimes we could think that since we don't feel bad about certain actions they must not be wrong, even though we know they violate basic principles of right behavior.

This is particularly common when someone has formed a habit of wrongdoing. After repeating a given activity a number of times, we may no longer feel that it is evil; our conscience no longer takes us to task for our conduct. We may even experience a feeling of power or accomplishment, for instance, after taking revenge on our enemy. But this doesn't lessen our responsibility, nor does it change the moral quality of our actions. It is simply an indication that our conscience has been deformed. Sometimes the opposite occurs, and we feel guilty when we have done nothing wrong (the case of a scrupulous conscience). But this, too, is a mistake.

The Role of Conscience

Is conscience, then, the awareness that we have done wrong? Actually that is just a part of the activity of the conscience. In fact, conscience acts in three distinct moments: (1) before we adopt a course of action, (2) while we are acting, and (3) after we have acted. Before we act the conscience serves to enlighten and counsel us. It reveals to us the moral quality of the action we are contemplating and consequently commands, forbids, or permits, depending on whether the action is right or wrong. While we are acting our conscience testifies that our action is moral or immoral, right or wrong. Finally, after we act the conscience judges what we have done, telling us if it was good or bad.

Conscience could be compared to physical pain. No one likes to feel pain, but it serves a very important function. Pain lets you know that you are harming yourself. Suppose you were to break your leg and feel no pain. You would continue going about your business but the injury would grow worse; perhaps the bone would set, but in a distorted position. In the same way, conscience tells you that damage has been done, that you are off course, so you have the chance to do something about it.

But conscience isn't only on the lookout for evil; more importantly, it encourages us to do good, to seek perfection in all we do. When an opportunity arises to assist an elderly person who's having trouble getting her groceries to her car, or to spend some time helping with the dishes, our conscience spurs us on to positive action.

FINE TUNING

When our conscience is healthy, it calls a spade a spade; it recognizes good as good and evil as evil — and doesn't confuse the two. But for different reasons our conscience can get maladjusted, like a scale that reads too heavy or too light. Most of us don't mind getting on a scale that reads light. It's nice to read "176 lbs." when you're really pushing 200. But if we want to know the truth, a faulty scale is a problem. Though we may read the scale correctly, we don't know what our true weight is.

To help distinguish a balanced conscience from one that's out of tune, we can use three adjectives to describe the degrees of sensitivity: scrupulous, lax, and well-formed.

1. *Scrupulous*: A scrupulous conscience is a sick conscience. Like the scale that reads too heavy, it makes everything appear worse than it is. It discovers sins where there are none and sees serious sin where there's merely imperfection. The scrupu-

lous conscience is timid and fearful. A scrupulous person interprets temptations as sin, even when there has been no consent of the free will. Living with a scrupulous conscience is similar to driving a car with the parking brake on: there is constant friction, tension, and stress.

A scrupulous conscience is a symptom of lack of confidence in the goodness and love of God. The surest cure for this moral sickness is to form our conscience correctly according to objective norms, and to take counsel from someone with proven good judgment.

2. *Lax*: At the opposite end of the spectrum we find the lax conscience — the scale that reads light. The person with a lax conscience decides on insufficient grounds that an evil action is permissible, or that something gravely wrong isn't so serious. He sees virtue where there is sin and perceives only flagrant deviations from the moral law.

The lax person has as his motto "To err is human," and convinces himself that either he's too weak to resist sin, or it simply doesn't matter. He is careless and makes light of wrongdoing with the excuse that "everyone does it, so it can't be so bad." This type of individual also tends to undervalue responsibility for his actions.

A lax conscience is like a stretched spring that has lost its elasticity. Through repeatedly acting *contrary* to what one knows is right in little things, or by ignoring its judgments, the conscience becomes dulled and insensitive. As Chesterton remarked, "One is tempted to say that a man who has not got a troubled conscience is in danger of having no conscience to be troubled."

3. *Well-formed*: The sensitive conscience falls at the midpoint between the two extremes. The well-formed conscience is *delicate* in the sense of attention to detail, like a painter with a delicate brush stroke, who isn't satisfied with general shapes and forms but insists on perfection.

A person whose conscience is well-formed is aware that he is before God at all times and doesn't allow himself to rationalize or hide from the truth. Moreover, a person with a sensitive conscience realizes that it's not enough to abstain from wrong actions, but actively pursues goodness in all he does.

MORAL OBLIGATION

As we have seen, there is more to conscience than a singing cricket in a top hat. It comes into play constantly as we chart the course of our lives as free human persons. In order to live in accord with right morality, it is necessary to embrace the two principal obligations of conscience: to form it and to obey it. Good will implies the resolve to conform to the objective rule which reason provides. Since our conscience is subject to error and needs to be educated, we also have the duty to form it.

Obedience to Conscience

It is often difficult to obey conscience. Thomas More, Chancellor of England, was beheaded by his good friend Henry VIII for refusing to take an oath recognizing Henry as head of the Church in England. It was a question of conscience. More often our difficulties come from within. Our passions, pride and selfishness pull us in the opposite direction of what we know we should do.

A particular difficulty for our times is the tendency to rationalize. If we can't perfectly understand the reason behind a certain obligation, we don't see why we should follow it. Yet there are countless things in life we don't fully understand and still accept. I cannot explain how magnetism works, or electricity, or gravitation, yet I know they work and are a reality of everyday life. Each time I flip on the lights I interact with a reality I do not fully understand but respect nonetheless. Moral truth is similar. It is always reasonable but at times surpasses my ability to understand it. My responsibility flows from a principle that I understand in itself, or which I accept from a source of authority to which I've freely committed myself.

Forming a Right Conscience

Conscience is not infallible, and errors in judgment do occur. Sometimes this is because one's conscience is poorly formed. It is possible, for example, for a child to be brought up with a false sense of values regarding some important moral questions, such as forgiveness of one's enemies, honesty, purity, or obedience to legitimate authority. Or even if a person has a sound set of values, he can make a mistake in applying his principles to a particular action. Because conscience is a human and imperfect judgment, it needs to be instructed — and sometimes corrected.

Each person should possess the degree of knowledge sufficient to live rightly in his or her own state in life. A doctor should be familiar with medical ethics, a married couple should know their duties towards each other and their children, a businessman ought to understand his ethical obligations towards his employees, and the principles of justice and charity. All of us should know the Ten Commandments, and the basic moral teaching of Christ and His Church. These objective principles form the *standard* against which our conscience can evaluate our actions.

A MATTER OF PERSPECTIVE

Conscience fundamentally determines the type of persons we are, the fruitfulness of our lives, and our personal holiness. It is more than just another aspect of life — especially for Christians. As Pope John Paul II explains in his encyclical letter *Redemptoris Missio*: "The Church's mission consists essentially in offering people an opportunity not to 'have more' but to 'be more,' *by awakening their consciences through the Gospel.*" This awakening takes the form of "opening one's eyes to the truth of one's existence."

Our attitude towards conscience is often a reflection of our attitude towards life. For many, conscience is a nuisance, a yoke they are forever trying to shake off. "It's that thing that keeps me from doing what I want, that thing that bothers me after I've done something wrong — why won't it just leave me in peace?" "So many people do it, and my conscience won't let me. . ." As Hamlet laments, "The sickly pale of thought over the native hue of resolution. . . thus conscience doth make cowards of us all."

This aversion to conscience is curious when we consider that we never complain about our other faculties, like having intelligence, or feelings, or the sense of smell or sight. No one gripes about having two legs or ten fingers. Why would some people like to do away with conscience? Perhaps it is because conscience seems to be something that, in short, won't allow them to enjoy evil. This isn't a very healthy outlook. Recognizing our guilt when we have done wrong is a logical consequence, like becoming ill after eating 24 White Castle hamburgers. If evil disturbs us, we should be pleased: it is a sign we have a healthy conscience. Seeking to do wrong without feeling remorse is not in harmony with the true meaning of life.

Others accept conscience for what it is: a gift. A person who really wants to do what is right finds in conscience an indispensable tool to help stay on the straight and narrow course. It is a question of intention. A driver who wants to wander off the road to do a little cross-country joyriding sees the guard rails on the side of the highway as a hindrance to his objective. Other drivers would express the opposite reaction: "Thank goodness there are painted lines and guard rails to help me stay on track."

It all depends on where you want to go. The will to live a good life is the bedrock of an upright conscience, and conscience is only appreciated by those who aspire to live according to the truth of their existence.

LEGALISM VS. LOVE

Our attitudes set the tone for our actions and color our reactions. Have you ever been with a person who really loves art? He can spend an hour contemplating a Renoir or a Monet that another might walk by without even noticing. A sunset or a colorful backyard scene fills him with an irresistible urge to run for a camera or a sketch pad and a box of oil pastels. His positive predisposition keeps him on perpetual "art-watch" and everything speaks to him of art.

We could ask ourselves: "What is my predisposition towards right and wrong? How enthusiastic am I about living a good life?" I think there are two main answers to this fundamental question. First we have those people whose goal in the moral field is to not break the rules. They're satisfied as long as they can manage to "keep their conscience clean." This attitude can be dubbed *moral legalism*. For this sort, morality is a code of laws, a set of rules to be obeyed, boundaries to stay within. Since one is always looking for the bare minimum, morality is summed up as what is "permitted" and what is "forbidden."

A prime flaw of moral legalism is that it blinds us to our omissions, all the good that we *could* be doing but aren't. We can become satisfied with doing nothing wrong, failing to realize that we're here on earth to do good. Or we could spend our lives doing many things that are not wrong in themselves, but which are essentially self-centered and do no good to anyone.

The essence of Christianity is more than the avoidance of evil: it is the imitation of Christ Who "went about doing good" (Acts 10:38). This reality brings to mind Christ's parable of the talents entrusted to three servants for them to administer and invest. When the master returned to see what profit each had made, he praised the first and second servants, but condemned the third because he had wasted his gifts and the opportunities he had to do good.

St. Paul did his utmost to change this legalistic mentality because it reflects a slave-to-master approach and undermines the true freedom of the children of God. He advocated the law of love instead of cold legalism. As we have seen, St. Augustine went so far as to sum up the moral law as "Love, and do as you please." We could think of the attitude of a mother caring for her sick child whom she loves. She isn't concerned just with doing her duty or merely fulfilling her parental obligations. Is she thinking, "What am I *required* to do for my child in this situation?" No! Motivated by love, she doesn't want to know the *minimum* she is obliged to do, but rather the *maximum* she can do for the good of her child. She looks for the most competent doctor, consults other parents, obtains the most effective medicines. Why? Because she is motivated by love and not mere obligation.

For those who want to love God authentically, for those who really want to be the best they can be, conscience is an invaluable guide for choosing the path of greater love and self-giving. It reminds us when we are letting up in the pursuit of our ideal and encourages us to tend ever higher. Few writers have expressed the power of love better than Thomas à Kempis in *The Imitation of Christ*:

> Love is a great thing, greatest of all goods, because it alone renders light every burden and bears without distinction every misfortune. Because it carries a burden without feeling it, and renders sweet and pleasing every bitterness.
> The lover flies, runs and rejoices; he is free and nothing can restrain him.
> Love feels no burden, values no labors, would like to do more than it can do, without excusing itself with impossibility, because it believes that all is lawful and possible for it to do.

In fact, it is ready to do anything, and it performs and effects many things in which he who does not love, faints and succumbs.

When fatigued it does not become tired; when pressed it does not work through constraint; when threatened it is not disturbed; but like a lively flame and a burning torch, it mounts upwards and securely overcomes all opposition.

Whoever loves knows well what this voice says.

In short, for those who live by love rather than legalism, conscience provides a sure orientation for the *right use* of freedom. And this is the most fundamental question of life's journey: *How* will I use the freedom I have?

Our answer to this question — expressed not in words but in actions — marks out the path we follow in life and, ultimately, the kind of persons we are.

CHAPTER 6

HARMONY OF
THE HUMAN PERSON

Attention to conscience opens the door to an authentic life. In William K. Kilpatrick's words, "Morality is not simply learning the rules of right and wrong, it is about a total alignment of ourselves." The human person is like a Rubik's cube: it is impossible to have just one square out of place. All the parts are interrelated and need to be harmonized if we are to reach our full potential. This self-alignment is commonly called maturity. A value is what perfects and completes the person, and maturity is a blending or synthesis of human values in an organic whole.

Everyone wants to be considered mature. One of the most stinging insults one can hurl at a 15-year-old is to call him or her immature. The great ambition of adolescents, along with being accepted by their peers, is to be regarded as grownup. Droves of young students fresh out of high school flock to college campuses every year to continue their education and get a taste of independence — the chance to determine their own destiny and be adults.

Maturity is a universal value, something all desire because of the image it expresses: "I'm mature, I'm independent, I know how to think for myself." But being *considered* mature and *being* mature are not identical. Once again we find that freedom not only doesn't exist without responsibility — it hinges on it.

People normally associate maturity with age — the older a person is, the more mature. Age indeed has something to do with maturity (our psychological, intellectual, physical and spiritual development occurs over time). Still, age is not *the* determining factor. There are irresponsible octogenarians just as there are mature 14-year-olds. A glimpse at current social problems is enough to assure us that not everyone over age 25 is truly mature.

We all have known cases that illustrate this unfortunate fact. A typical example is a middle-aged man who leaves his wife and children for a younger woman. Our immediate reaction to cases like this is incredulity, pain and anger. ("What a senseless thing to do!" "His poor wife and kids!" "What a jerk!") Besides the obvious moral implications, we can only say that here there is an acute lack of the most basic human maturity.

What we have is an adolescent in a grey,

three-piece suit with all the outward appearance of an adult.

MATURITY MYTHS

Popular culture attributes to maturity elements which don't correspond to its true nature. Three common myths are often interwoven into our modern notions of maturity: (1) invulnerability, (2) infallibility, and (3) inflexibility.

First, maturity is not *invulnerability*. Our society sometimes presents maturity as freedom from all temptation and wrongdoing, as if right and wrong were something for children. Adults are made to feel that they are supposed to be (to use one of Nietzsche's expressions) *"jenseits von Gut und Bösen,"* beyond good and evil. We need only think of the signs posted in movie theaters and newspapers to advertise pornographic movies: "For mature audiences only" — as if concern for moral living were solely a matter for children. The truth, of course, is the opposite. An adult is mature precisely because he doesn't need someone else to tell him to do what's right or to keep him from doing wrong. He acts on personal convictions and right conscience.

Mature persons recognize their weakness. They avoid occasions of wrongdoing and look for opportunities to do good. "Fools rush in where angels fear to tread," as Alexander Pope would put it.

To think of maturity as invulnerability is like saying a person can't be harmed by a power-saw because he's mature. An adult is able to use power tools precisely because he is aware of the danger and takes the necessary precautions to stay out of harm's way.

A second error is to conceive of maturity as *infallibility*. Maturity doesn't mean we have all the answers. Far from it. Socrates said that the wisest man is the one who recognizes his own ignorance. The more mature a person is, the more humble he will be in recognizing his personal limitations. "Humility," in the words of St. Teresa of Avila, "is truth." No more and no less. And the truth is that each of us is capable of error. The mature person recognizes his own weakness and is not hasty in judging. He ponders, studies, consults and decides with prudence.

A third error concerning maturity is to associate it with *inflexibility*. Some mistakenly think of maturity as a permanent state of seriousness and stiffness, the inability to laugh, to enjoy simple things, to take things lightly. The beauty of maturity is its harmony. To laugh, converse, appreciate other people and the wonders of nature —these are beautiful human qualities and are signs of maturity.

The person who is truly mature knows when

it's time to be serious and when it's time to take things lightly. His life isn't carried away by super-ficiality but rather is guided by clear principles. The poetic verses at the beginning of the third chapter of the book of Ecclesiastes are a fine synopsis of the balance that maturity provides.

> For everything there is a season,
> and a time for every purpose under heaven:
> a time to be born, and a time to die. . .
> a time to break down, and a time to build
>   up. . .
> a time to weep, and a time to laugh. . .
> a time to mourn, and a time to dance. . .
> a time to keep silence, and a time to
>   speak. . .

Maturity is being able to discern between one time and another, knowing what is right for every occasion.

In Search of a Definition

Having seen what maturity is not, we turn to what it is. The word means different things in different circumstances. If we turn on the television in the early evening we might have the good fortune to catch a rerun of *The Wild, Wild World of Animals*, in which William Conrad could inform us that a mature male grizzly bear can weigh up to

1500 pounds. On another occasion a good friend might tell us she's met a wonderful man who is so mature. We find the word in a variety of settings with slightly different shades of meaning. For this reason we will propose three definitions, rather than one.

Perfection of One's Nature

In the broadest sense of the term, maturity is the consummation or perfection of one's nature, the high point of a growth process when something becomes what it was meant to be. This is a one-directional process — progress, not just change. When something matures it becomes more and more what it *should be*, not just more and more something else.

A dog is most a dog at the peak of its development, at maturity. Before that point it's a puppy; afterwards it's an old dog (you know, the kind you can't teach any new tricks). An apple is most an apple when it is ripe. In fact, in many languages the word used for "mature" is the same word used for "ripe." In German a ripe apple is *ein reifer Apfel* and a mature person is *ein reifer Mensch*. Likewise in French a ripe pomegranate is *une grenade mûre* while a mature woman is *une femme mûre*.

In this sense maturity can apply to plants, animals, human beings, even wine — anything that undergoes an organic development. This definition also holds true for our physical nature. A young person grows and reaches maturity; then the body begins to deteriorate. Hence the expression, over the hill — the hill being one's prime, the pinnacle of (physical) development.

But unlike apples and grizzly bears, human beings have a spiritual nature as well, and it is here that maturity takes on its uniquely human dimension. For there is much more to human maturity than the peak of bodily growth. In all other material creatures maturity is strictly a physical phenomenon; human maturity is physical, emotional, psychological and spiritual.

Internalization of Principles

According to a more specific definition, maturity refers to the transformation of external norms and rules into internal principles and convictions. This process of assimilation should be conscious and free, as a person gradually learns to recognize and appreciate certain values.

Children have to be watched, reminded (in some cases even forced) to do their homework or go to church on Sunday. Their parents have to regulate the amount of television they watch because they don't have enough maturity to discipline themselves or to discern what is best. Any little girl or boy, if they were the ones to plan their diet, would sooner eat chocolate cake than green beans for dinner. Norms must be imposed from outside because children follow their natural inclinations and impressions and are not usually very capable of thinking things through or sacrificing an immediate pleasure for a future good. These qualities are proper of an adult.

In the same way, a young person who goes away to college and wastes his time, who doesn't follow a study program, who leaves aside moral living to follow his passions and natural tendencies can in no way be considered mature. He is like unripe fruit.

Who is around to see him, what his friends do or don't do, what people will think of him — these things carry less weight for a mature individual, because he's in charge of his own life. He follows the principles and convictions that he has freely made his own.

Harmony of the Human Person

Human maturity in its fullest sense is harmony of the person. Rather than a single quality it is a condition formed by many and varied qualities: a compendium of values rather than an isolated value. We could compare maturity to a work of art, an exquisite oil painting — a Rembrandt or a Velázquez. The colors blend perfectly. Everything fits together — the lines, the shapes and forms, the proportion and perspective. Every brush stroke is important and every color necessary to complete and perfect the work.

The same can be said of maturity. It is harmony and proportion, the blending and integration of many different human qualities into an organic whole: will, intellect, emotions, memory, imagination — all the faculties that constitute the human person. Its not enough that all elements be present; there must be order and harmony among them. All the artist's colors are present on the palette — but the palette isn't the work of art.

This harmony takes the form of a perfect correspondence between what one *is* and what one *professes to be*, and its most convincing expression is fidelity in living out one's commitments. In a mature person there is no place for hypocrisy, no room for insincerity.

Just as an apple is most an apple when it's ripe, and a dog is most truly a dog when in its prime, so a person is most human when he is mature.

Unlike other creatures, we, as human beings, are able to reflect on our nature, and because we are free we can decide to live (or not live) in accordance with what we were made to be. Maturity, then, is agreement between the way we live and our true nature.

Among other things, this implies acceptance of our state in life and living in conformity with all its demands. If we are married and we are mature, we live according to the nature of the married state. We probably won't act the same way as we would if we were single — active social life, staying late at work, taking trips at a moment's notice. Our habits, pastimes, relationships with other people, and the use of our time — all these things will be ordered according to the commitment we have freely assumed when we got married. To do otherwise would be to live a lie. We would be saying that we are one thing while acting like another.

Maturity means embracing the joys and hardships implied in our decisions, as we find expressed in the lifelong promise of a husband and wife on their wedding day: "For better or for worse, for richer, for poorer, in sickness and in health, till death do us part." Mature people are able to commit themselves without fear, because they are masters of their own persons and not slaves to changing circumstances.

A LIGHT GENERATION

In 1992 the noted Spanish psychiatrist and author, Enrique Rojas, published a book entitled *El hombre light* ("Light Man"). He compares the wave of light products that hit the market in the '80's — caffeine-free Coca-Cola, alcohol-free beer, cholesterol-free margarine and sugar-free sweeteners — with a new type of person lacking substance, all façade with nothing inside. "Light" is in, and with it a whole new way of looking at life: everything light, weak, reduced, watered down, devoid of content.

Rojas asserts that with the new psychological climate a new model of person has arisen: the "Light Man." He can be described as follows. He is indifferent to transcendent values, holding on to nothing but money, power, success, sex, narcissism and a good time as the sum and substance of life. He no longer has firm beliefs nor accepts absolute truth —though he has an insatiable desire for information. He wants to know everything, not to change or better himself, but just to be aware of what's going on.

The "Light Man" corresponds to what C.S. Lewis calls "men without chests." The chest (seat of character, principle and magnanimity) is the "indispensable liaison officer between the cerebral man and the visceral man." Without principle, we abandon what is most human in us. A superabundance of data and statistics in no way makes up for a lack of principle and character. Nor is the rationalist more intelligent than anyone else. As Lewis observes, "Their heads are no bigger than the ordinary: it is the atrophy of the chest beneath that makes them seem so."

Four principal characteristics are attributed to the "Light Man": hedonism, consumerism, permissiveness, and relativism. He suffers from a surfeit of "things" and a corresponding dearth of "values." Fed up and bored with life, he searches for happiness *à la carte*. His thought is weak and inconsistent, his convictions wobbly. As a whole, the "Light Man" is a person without a reference point. He has no fixed goal nor meaning for his undertakings.

Contrasting this fragile new sort of man, Rojas introduces *el hombre sólido* — "Solid Man." While the "Light Man" advances in everything except what is most essential, the "Solid Man" commits himself, strives to be consistent, deep, and morally true. He overcomes the reigning cynical skepticism and is capable of being spiritual, discovering the beautiful, the noble and the great that are present in existence.

The "Solid Man" is a mature person. His life has direction and his actions fit in to the meaning of his existence as a whole. Maturity is solidity. Maturity is having ideals and standing by them. In somewhat different terms, Fr. Marcial Maciel, founder of the Legionaries of Christ, describes this disparity between the mature and immature:

> History and the modern mentality have accustomed us to classifying men as either good or bad, smart or stupid, rich or poor — but I believe there is a more basic distinction, a distinction more in conso-

nance with what the human person is. I would separate people as generous or selfish, those who struggle and those who passively follow their senses. Selfishness and magnanimity, sensuality and struggle have divided the world into two bands that pervade every race, culture, age and social structure. In the final analysis one can be materially the poorest person in the world and the least intelligent, but if there is generosity and a spirit of work and conquest, there we have a man whose center of reference is above himself, a person who has taken life seriously and aspires to an ideal. . . If this person becomes filled with love for Christ, if we offer him a transcendent ideal, if we invite him to cultivate the life of grace, we have a saint.

One such man was St. Thomas More. In 1960 the British playwright Robert Bolt wrote the brilliant drama *A Man for All Seasons*, subsequently made into a film that won the Oscar for Best Picture in 1966. Bolt — himself a non-Christian — was so captivated by St. Thomas More's strength of character that he made him the object of his study and his art.

Bolt, like Rojas and Lewis, perceived the modern phenomenon of *el hombre light*. "It is with us as it is with our cities," he comments in the preface of his play, "— an accelerating flight to the periphery, leaving a centre which is empty when the hours of business are over." He was taken with Thomas More's solidity in the face of a society fraught with "lightness." "What first attracted me," he writes, "was a person who could not be accused of any incapacity for life, who indeed seized life in great variety and greedy quantities, who nevertheless found something in himself without which life was valueless and when that was denied him was able to grasp his death."

This, then, is the basic difference dividing humanity. *Solid* or light, *mature* or immature, egoistic or *open to others*. We will have to examine more closely the characteristics of these two types.

WHEN I WAS A CHILD. . .

If you ever get the chance to visit the Louvre in Paris, the Uffizi Palace in Florence or any number of churches in Rome, you will surely come upon one of Caravaggio's oil paintings. His *chiaroscuro* masterpieces are a testimony to the force of contrast. Light and dark are never so apparent as when found side-by-side. Concepts likewise often become clearer when contrasted with their opposites. To clarify our ideas on maturity we can compare it to its opposite: "childishness." Maturation is, in effect, the passage from childhood into adulthood.

In writing to the Corinthians, St. Paul reflects on this process in his own life. "When I was a child I used to talk like a child, think like a child, and reason like a child. When I became a man, I put childish ways aside" (1 Cor 13:11). He later adds a distinction: "Brothers, do not be children in judgment. Be children in evil, but mature men in judgment" (1 Cor 14:20).

Being like a child is not all bad. On several occasions Christ exhorted His disciples to be like children, to the point of making it a condition for entering Heaven. "I assure you, unless you change and become like little children, you will not enter the Kingdom of Heaven" (Mt 18:3). It is appropriate to qualify the word "child," since it has two radically different connotations. To be *childlike* is to be simple, trusting, innocent and open — all the positive traits of childhood. In this sense, we must *strive* to be children. To be *childish*, on the other hand, is to be puerile, selfish, and naive — in short, immature.

By considering ten pairs of contrasting characteristics, we can zero in on a fairly precise understanding of maturity. The first term of each pair is associated with childishness, the second with maturity. The chart presents a synthesis of these qualities.

	Child	Adult
1	Superficiality	Depth
2	Impulsiveness	Reflection
3	Instability	Constancy
4	Sentiment	Character
5	Immediate satisfaction	Capacity for sacrifice
6	Self-importance	Humility
7	Subjectivity	Objectivity
8	Extremes	Balance
9	Egoism	Openness
10	Dependence	Independence

1. Superficiality vs. Depth

Superficial comes from the Latin word *superficies*, which means "surface." Superficiality = shallowness. It refers to a preoccupation with externals without penetrating the substance of things. A superficial person has more concern for *appearances* than for reality.

Children tend to be superficial. A child lives from moment to moment, his life being a series of discoveries and experiences. When one adventure ends he's on to the next. He doesn't look beneath the surface to discover a connection between events or an underlying meaning to his experiences. He is satisfied to take things as they come. This shallowness in his outlook grants him a refreshing innocence, but also leads him to judge by appearances and first impressions. Children are excellent observers, but often poor interpreters of others' words and actions.

Shallowness isn't limited to children. A good friend of mine recently returned from a visit to his family, who live abroad and whom he hadn't seen for a number of years. His younger brother, now 29, zips around city streets at upwards of ninety miles per hour in his sports car. As soon as he pays it off, he plans to sell it and buy a motorcycle. His sister spends an average of three months of the year touring around Europe with a group of bicyclists who make merry with the people they come across. My friend was distressed because, as he put it, "They see no sense to their lives other than to have a good time while it lasts."

A mature person is characterized by depth. He looks for *meaning* beyond information; he looks for *reality* beyond appearance. This concern to get to the bottom of things leads to a correct evaluation of persons, ideas and situations. Depth implies a realistic outlook, free from prejudice and superficial criticism. A mature person looks reality in the face and deals with it as it is.

"Reality" does not mean merely what is visible or perceptible by our external senses. There is no reason to suppose that what is invisible is necessarily less real than what is visible. Love is no less real than pottery. God is no less real than His creatures. In fact, He is infinitely more real. All creatures come into existence and many will one day cease to exist. But God has neither beginning nor end.

2. *Impulsiveness vs. Reflection*

One consequence of superficiality is *impetu-osity*. Since a superficial person perceives only what is immediately apparent, he doesn't foresee the consequences of his actions. He acts on the spur of the moment. I remember an accident that happened to a young boy who lived down the street from me when I was a child. After putting a firecracker in a bottle he looked inside to see why it hadn't exploded, and in that moment it did. Fortunately the doctors were able to save his eye, but his vision was permanently impaired. This is a typical example of the recklessness that follows from a lack of reflection.

The virtue opposed to impulsiveness is *re-flection*: the habit of thinking things through before acting. Because he considers well before making his decisions, the mature person is more certain he won't have to regret them afterwards. This holds for everything from business deals to course selection at college to the choice of a vocation or the right spouse.

At the same time, reflection is not indecisive-ness. We can never have total assurance or take into account all factors and possible consequences of our actions. Prudence is balance.

Reflection comes into play for words as well as actions. How much suffering is caused by harsh words and thoughtless comments! As St. James said, "The one who doesn't sin with his tongue is a perfect man" (Jm 3:2). Reflection saves us from many regrets.

3. Instability vs. Constancy

Feelings are volatile. If they are allowed to rule our decisions they lead to inconstancy. One of the most typical characteristics of children is the brevity of their attention span. A child begins to put a puzzle together, then five minutes later he is tired of that and starts playing with his toy car. Mom's purse suddenly catches his eye and he's off to explore its contents. There is as yet no principle to tie his activities together.

The same phenomenon can be observed among immature adults. They are inconstant and lack tenacity in seeing projects through to the end. A person who has never achieved maturity is irresponsible and often can't hold down a job, because he cannot be counted on to get his work done. He needs supervision to ensure he keeps working and doesn't get into trouble by following his whims.

The ability to make and be faithful to personal commitments is true freedom, and a mature person is free. If one is mature, he is able to make responsible choices without regretting them afterward. This responsibility in turn affords stability to his life.

When a mature person has made a life decision he doesn't keep reconsidering his choice year after year: "Was it all a mistake? Maybe I didn't know what I was doing; I was so young. I think I don't love her anymore. . ." The attitude of a mature individual is quite different: "I knew that not everything was going to be easy. Difficulties and sacrifices are part of the package, and they're worth it. What matters is to be faithful." This second outlook frees us from the ups and downs of our changing moods.

Sometimes tenacity is undervalued. In a 1993 issue of *US News & World Report*, John Leo laments the campaign to remove competitive sports from schools so as to avoid traumas among the students. As Leo argues, the success of this campaign would be a misfortune for the country.

Sports teach the virtue of determination, stick-to-itiveness, teamwork and valor. Learning to lose and learning to win, learning to get up when you've fallen, to pick up your tools and begin all over again — this virtue has been chiefly responsible for the greatest personal and cooperative achievements of mankind. The Duke of Wellington has often been quoted as saying that "the battle of Waterloo was won on the playing fields of Eton."

There are ideals worth fighting for. Even those who are striving to get competitiveness out of schools cannot hope to succeed in their agenda if they do not exhibit resolve, perseverance and tenacity.

Constancy implies self-discipline. Work inevitably becomes tedious at times, and distractions and other options are always a temptation. But a mature person never leaves anything unfinished except in cases of necessity; a work begun is a work completed. Seeing a project through to the end is far more difficult than just starting with enthusiasm. Aesop's tale of the Tortoise and the Hare — as valid today as when it was written — testifies to the eminent value of perseverance. Slow and steady wins the race.

4. Sentiment vs. Character

Character is like a T-bone steak: solid and substantial. Sentiment is like the A-1 sauce that goes on top: an accessory. It is important to keep these two in their proper places. Sentiment is made up of passing moods, impressions and feelings, whereas character is made up of principles and a firm will.

Children tend to follow their feelings and urges. They don't need to be told, "If it feels good, do it" — they do this naturally. Their moods and inclinations rule.

An immature person is like a leaf in the wind or a weather vane blown this way and that with no clear purpose or fundamental orientation. Have you seen a dried leaf on a blustery day? One minute a gust of wind carries it to a sunny hilltop, the next minute it deposits it in the mud. Something similar occurs to an immature person at the mercy of his unpredictable whims.

For a mature adult, reason and will reign over moods and feelings. He is able to act contrary to his feelings. This doesn't mean a contempt for emotions or a blind repression of sentiments. It is not a matter of "either/or" but "which directs which." We needn't repress either feelings or reason, but one of the two must take the upper hand. Principle should never be compromised by feelings. Habitual subordination of our emotions to the direction and interpretation of reason and will frees us from living as slaves to our impulses, feelings and impressions.

Some would see this as a threat to "spontaneity." Our generation puts a premium on the ability to be relaxed and off-the-cuff. "We have to take things as they come, with flexibility. . ."

Still, spontaneity isn't appropriate in every circumstance. We appreciate spontaneity in an informal chat or in times of recreation. But for most of us, spontaneity isn't one of the things we look for in our surgeon or accountant. The thought of a spontaneous experiment in the middle of open-heart surgery doesn't inspire much confidence. In these and many other cases we would prefer professionalism to gratuitous creativity, ingenuity and spontaneity. The key is to know how to act in every situation — and this requires self-dominion.

A mature person is authentic — that is, the real, interior person is the one who runs the show. There are two different ways of understanding "authenticity." Some see it as the unhindered expression of one's instinctive impulses, free from any restraint. This vitalistic understanding of authenticity falls well short of the mark, making human beings out to be no more than animals.

The other way of understanding authenticity takes into account our spiritual nature as creatures made in the image and likeness of God. Our tendencies and aspirations are examined by our conscience, which approves of or rejects them. In this sense, authenticity is not the spontaneous expression of impulses, but an ideal to be conquered. It is an effort to live according to the truth of our being and the authentic meaning of our life.

5. *Immediate Satisfaction vs. Capacity for Sacrifice*

A child's world is the present and thus he is naturally impatient. Johnny doesn't merely want the cookie — he wants it *now*. Try telling a child he has to wait before going out to play — you might as well tell him he will *never* play. Since he lives by sensations, a child is unable to think ahead and plan for the future. That's why having a child save up coins in a piggy bank is such a healthy preparation for adult life.

An individual is mature if he knows how to put what he *should* do above what he *feels* like doing. Often parents don't feel like feeding their children, cleaning up after them, and caring for their needs but, fortunately for the children, there are many unselfish parents.

Sacrifice has never been a popular topic. When Jesus announced to His disciples that "if anyone wants to come after Me, let him deny himself, take up his cross every day and follow Me," the disciples were undoubtedly squirming in their tunics. Sacrifice isn't likable. Not only that, it has no value in and of itself. It does have value, however, in three instances, and the mature person recognizes this.

- *As a means to achieve an objective.* Every choice entails renunciation but only because by our choice we're obtaining something better. A student, for instance, gives up some years of his life to prepare himself to reap the benefits later.
- *As exercise to form the will.* There are some

qualities that can only be acquired by practice. Willpower is one of them. Like a football player, you can only learn so much from books and then it's time to hit the playing field for hours of drills. Self-denial is an indispensable drill for the will.

- *As an act of love.* A sacrifice made for someone else is like saying, "See, I love you even more than I love myself. I prefer you to myself." Every gift is a sort of sacrifice, a piece of self that we offer to the other.

The ability to overcome ourselves and do what is difficult strengthens our character and allows us to make something of our lives. Every great work and lasting project, including the project of building an authentic personality, requires willpower and the capacity for sacrifice.

6. Exaggerated Self-Importance vs. Humility

In many circumstances children may be either rash or overly cautious. They haven't yet acquired a realistic view of their own capabilities and limitations. We often discover these same traits in immature persons, who never quite adjust to reality.

Humility is self-knowledge and self-acceptance, the recognition of one's qualities and limitations. A person is mature when he has an objective view of himself, thinking neither more nor less of himself than what he really is. Honest self-knowledge is the starting point to make something of one's life.

A humble person is also able to recognize the good in others. He is secure enough to appreciate sound traditions and doesn't exaggerate the value of his own "creativity." On this subject, Richard John Neuhaus has written:

> Creativity requires humility, which is the discipleship of apprenticing oneself to the past. The creativity of the ignorant and unpracticed is nothing more than "self-expression," which is, regrettably, what many mean by creativity today. A bawling child is engaged in self-expression. Adults who demand attention for their self-expression assume, usually without warrant, that they have very interesting selves to express. Truly interesting people are people who understand themselves to be serving a tradition, and interesting traditions are traditions that aspire to a truth or good beyond themselves.

7. Subjectivity vs. Objectivity

The subjectivity with which children view themselves is symptomatic of a more general subjectivism. A child's world is very small. Reality for him is the reality of his personal experience and impressions of things.

As he grows up, a child must learn to be objective in his assessment of situations. This habit, together with that of reflection, will help him avoid rash judgments. A mature person penetrates the heart of the matter and after considering the various factors is able to make a fair, balanced evaluation.

This fairness is particularly necessary in dealing with other people. They deserve the benefit of the doubt and not a hasty condemnation. A good motto in our personal relationships is: "Believe all the good you hear; believe only the evil you see."

Another facet of objectivity is the ability to see things from another's point of view. It is not easy to leave aside one's prejudices and long-held opinions to consider the validity of someone else's position, but this frees us from subjectivism and makes us more impartial in our judgment.

8. Extremism vs. Balance

Children are quick to pass categorical judgments. Everything is black or white and there are only good guys and bad guys. In reality most of us are some shade of grey, and we all are capable of heroic deeds and the most abhorrent crimes.

Unfortunately this infantile way of labelling things and people is often carried into later life.

One is mature when he has learned to discover the good in everyone, to excuse others' faults and cultivate his own capacity for goodness.

Since maturity is harmony, a mature individual knows what is important and what can be taken lightly. Mature parents emphasize what is most necessary in raising their children. Some things don't merit a lot of attention. Other matters — such as the education of their children, their faith and moral life, justice and charity — are never passed over.

Aristotle taught that virtue is a midpoint between two extremes. He described courage, for example, as the just mean between cowardice and recklessness. The coward flees from danger; the reckless man rushes headlong into it. The courageous man faces danger when he must, without giving in to fear.

Yet it is also important not to confuse this balance with mediocrity. To seek the just mean is not lukewarmness. The person who prays every day and takes eternity into account in his daily decisions isn't a religious fanatic. He's a realist. A mature person puts emphasis where it belongs: on what is most important in life.

9. Egoism vs. Openness to Others

Small children are the center of their own particular universe. Everything revolves around their needs and desires, and they are unable to put others before themselves.

Immaturity is accompanied by egotism. An immature person tends to get caught up with himself and his own concerns, which makes it difficult for him to think of others. Thus he has trouble understanding others, feeling compassion for what they suffer, or sharing in their joy.

Maturity, on the other hand, is marked by openness and genuine concern for others. It is the ability to forget oneself and put others in the first place.

A 7-year-old girl complains when she has to receive a necessary injection because she knows it is going to hurt. She would do anything to avoid it. Yet we may find the same girl at the age of 17 voluntarily giving blood at the local Red Cross center because she knows her sacrifice could save someone's life. This is the difference maturity makes.

10. Dependence vs. Independence

Peer-pressure is the plague of adolescents. Children often pass through periods of insecurity and thirst for acceptance from those around them. This is natural in youngsters, but catastrophic if carried into later life. An immature person is afraid of what others will think or say. If he lacks the strength to stand up for his principles, he will act one way when he is alone, another way with one group of friends, and another way with others.

The mature person, on the other hand, is consistent, acting the same when people are around and when they're not. He draws from within himself the meaning and direction of his actions, instead of taking them from the popular standards of the world. An important lesson in life is to learn to be who we are, with consistency between how we act and what we profess to be.

A mature person's independence from the environment has another dimension. He is able to question the values society presents. It is representative of this type of person not to believe everything he hears. Of course it is not a sign of maturity to believe nothing at all; this is cynicism. A mature individual considers what is being said, who is saying it and why. He tests the values he is offered against tried and true principles. As we read in the letter to the Hebrews, "Solid food is for mature men with minds trained by practice to distinguish between good and bad" (Heb 5:14).

After reviewing these ten principles we could be left a little numb, with a feeling of despair at the prospect of putting them into practice. Studying maturity is one thing — living it is quite another. Is it humanly possible to live as a mature person?

Fortunately there are mature people around that give us good — even heroic — example. We could return to January, 1993, to the city of

Bergamo, Italy. There a young woman named Carla Levati died eight hours after giving birth to Stefano, her second son. During her pregnancy doctors had diagnosed a tumor and advised her to have an abortion. She refused. Her response to those who tried to persuade her to undergo radiation therapy was, "One day less of my life is one day more for my child."

Her husband, Valerio, is a carpenter. His modest response to the hordes of reporters who came to question him about the affair was, "I don't know about these things. In my life I only learned how to hammer nails into wood." But in a tattered notebook that served as Valerio's diary one finds this simple entry, "Thank you, Carla, because you have made me a complete man. I'm happy because Stefano is born. Congratulations, Carla. Thank you. Good-bye." Despite the bad news that makes the daily headlines, heroes are still to be found in our world.

THE PATTERN TO FOLLOW

When a Christian wants to know where true maturity is to be found, if he's looking for a model to see how it should be done, he doesn't have to look far. Jesus Christ, the perfect man, is the center and model of Christian life. He has left us an example of consummate maturity that invites us to imitation.

On considering Christ's life we are immediately struck with His profound sense of personal identity. He knows Who He is and what He is about. On coming into the world His attitude is summed up in the words, "Here I am, Lord, I come to do Your will." His whole life is a continuous living out of that identity, so much so that He derives His very nourishment from His fidelity: "My food is to do the will of Him who sent Me and to bring His work to completion" (Jn 4:34).

Jesus never succumbs to popular opinion. When the crowds, overwhelmed by His teachings and miracles, want to carry Him off to make Him king, He slips away quietly, because His hour has not yet come.

And when His hour finally does arrive, He embraces the Father's will and freely surrenders Himself up to death, though His human nature resists in the face of such suffering. Nowhere else could we hope to find such a perfect example of maturity. Christ's life is an open book that reveals to us the truth about ourselves and marks out the path that we are to follow.

A truly integrated, mature personality is an ideal that is worth working for. In modern society where "having" often receives preference over authentic "being," examples of maturity are desperately needed. Only by living according to the truth of our being will we discover the path to true and lasting happiness.

Chapter 7

IN PURSUIT OF HAPPINESS

Buying gifts for others is seldom an easy task — especially when we don't know the other person well. Perhaps that's why there are books published on the subject to keep us from making some gaffe in our selection. "Let's see... I could buy her a fern, but then again she might not like plants and for all I know she could be allergic..." "I could get him an Armani necktie, but he probably has all the ties he needs and who knows what style he prefers..." "Ah! Maybe a nice bottle of Grand Marnier — but then again, what if he's a teetotaler?" The trick is to choose something that absolutely everyone would like to have, but hasn't yet acquired.

We seem to have overcome this problem in greeting cards and the well-wishes we exchange on important celebrations. "Merry Christmas! Happy New Year! Happy Birthday! Happy 25th Anniversary! Happy Mothers Day!" It's happy this and happy that, regardless of what we are celebrating. These good wishes are usually gratefully received (except, of course, by the Ebenezer

Scrooge types) because happiness is the one thing we know everyone wants and can't seem to get enough of.

How does this tie in with human values? Happiness is the queen of values, the pot of gold at the end of the rainbow. We all want it, so it clearly is appreciated. And is it a good for us? As we saw in chapter 2, we are made to be happy. This is our destiny — to be happy forever. Moreover, all our other actions have happiness as their end. Happiness isn't a *means* for anything. It is not a tool or a stepping stone to anything else. No one uses happiness to get more money or more pleasure. We want money or pleasure because we think they are going to make us happy.

IS EVERYBODY HAPPY?

Then why are our efforts at achieving happiness such a flop? It seems that few people are really happy. An article that appeared in *Time* magazine (September 13, 1993) was subtitled: "Contentment is. . . pretty hard to find anywhere you go these days — or so say a bevy of international pollsters."

There are many who laugh and wallow in distractions, amusements and entertainment, but they don't seem to have conquered happiness. Often it appears they are running from themselves. We can see this in our modern distaste for silence. We fill our world with noise and music, with one activity after another, but rarely do we dare to take a moment to reflect on our life and where we're going.

There are books and books written about happiness — from ancient philosophers to pop psychologists — and still people don't seem to get any happier. Walk down the sidewalks of Paris or New York City or London. Look intently into the eyes of the people you pass. Are most of them happy? It doesn't seem so much of the time. Read the newspapers. Ask your neighbors and co-workers if they're truly happy. The tragic fact of the matter is, most people really aren't very happy.

Sometimes we are misled into thinking that there is a whole gamut of material elements without which we can never be happy. "You can never be happy without a lot of money, power, assorted pleasures, experiences, etc." These are the requirements for happiness propagated by popular culture. The United Nations once went so far as to formulate a 12-point list of requirements for being happy that included a radio, a bicycle, and a set of kitchen utensils per family.

Linking happiness to material possessions and good fortune is disconcerting. These conditions are external to us, and, to a certain extent, beyond our control. More importantly, none of them is permanent or secure. If I can't be secure in my possession of these prerequisites for happiness, then I can never be truly happy. I will always live in the anguish of knowing that my happiness is as precarious as a house of cards, liable to collapse at a moment's notice. Moreover, the human experience does not support this connection. There are materially poor people who are extremely happy, just as there are wretched millionaires.

We in the modern age are like spoiled children — inundated with "things," but deeply unsatisfied. Civilization offers us a cornucopia of consumer goods that our recent ancestors never dreamed of. Yet we live more anguished and miserable lives than people in past decades. We know how to make an airplane, how to go to the moon; we know how an automobile and a computer work. But we feel immensely unhappy because we don't know how we ourselves work, what we are for, what the *meaning* of our existence is. Technological progress provides us with ever more answers to our "whats," "hows," and "whens," but our "whys" go unanswered.

Nietzsche once wrote, "Whoever has a *why* to live will always find a *how*." "Whys" deal with meaning, and meaning is necessary for happiness. The problem is, we have all the "hows" today but have neglected the more important "why?"

What is the solution to this distressing situation? What can we do to become happier ourselves and to help others be happier? Happiness is elusive. It escapes our grasp not only because we don't know how to acquire it, but because we often don't even know *what* it is. A first step, then, will be to consider well what happiness *is*, since there are many theories of happiness floating around. Our answer must be linked in some way to our previous look at human nature.

Most of us would have a hard time defining happiness. A major complication is that there are different types of happiness. To say, "I feel happy" after drinking a glass of wine does not mean the same as "Jeff is a happy person" or "Ellen and John are happily married." We will need to distinguish between these different types or degrees of happiness.

Degrees of Happiness

The succulent *Churrascao* is one of the hallmarks of Brazilian culinary culture. After soaking in a mixture of vinegar, salt and other herbs and spices, a choice cut of beef is slow-roasted over a charcoal fire. The longer the meat is left immersed in the mixture, the more deeply the flavor of the spices permeates the beef. It depends on how much we want the flavor to penetrate.

Something similar occurs in the case of happiness. There are different "degrees of penetration." Happiness can be superficial and passing, or go to the core of our being. By clarifying four basic degrees of happiness, it will be easier to see how this word can have different meanings in different contexts.

1st Degree: Bliss*

All of us have experienced moments of bliss, euphoria, and emotional pleasure. There are moments when we sit back, forget our troubles and bask in a feeling of "letting go." These feelings flow from a wide range of sources. Anything from a bike ride to a sing-along with friends around a campfire to lying on your back in the grass staring up at a midnight sky, teeming with sparkling stars. They can even be produced artificially, for instance by drugs or alcohol.

Simon and Garfunkel's *The 59th Street Bridge Song* sums up an attitude typical of the sixties and, in a certain way, attractive to all of us:

> Slow down, you're movin' too fast,
> You got to make the mornin' last,
> Just kickin' down the cobblestones,
> Lookin' for fun and feelin' groovy. . .
>
> I got no deeds to do, no promises to keep,
> I'm dappled and drowsy and ready to sleep,

---

* I use this term with reluctance, for lack of a better expression. In its original and proper meaning, bliss refers to the supreme happiness of Heaven. Here I use it in its colloquial sense of "happy oblivion."

Let the morning time drop all its petals on me,
Life I love you, all is groovy.

"Feelin' groovy" — which would correspond roughly to the Eagles' "peaceful, easy feeling" — is a superficial sort of happiness, deliberately out of touch with reality. We forget our concerns and commitments and escape to feelings of easygoing and untrammeled freedom, like a raft drifting lazily down a quiet river. "Feelin' groovy" takes on two different modes, one more active (euphoria), and the other passive (carefree contentment). This type of happiness appeals to a lower level of our being. It bypasses our higher faculties (the intelligence and the will) and heads straight for the sensory level of our nature: the imagination, external senses, and feelings.

That's okay — as long as the means are licit, a little escape now and again can do us good — but we should avoid confusing these occasions with true happiness. Experience confirms that the rolling brook of frivolity often lets out into the ocean of existential angst.

This is the manner of happiness promised by pop cults, New Age and MTV. A life of meaning is cashed in for a stream of sensations and experiences. In the end they leave the mind and soul parched and dried out like an over-cooked pork chop. This is not the kind of happiness that satisfies the deeper desires within us.

2nd Degree: Gladness

Sometimes you just wake up on the right foot. There are days when everything comes up roses. The first day of vacation, a raise at work, a $300 win at the horse races... You've got the world by the tail. These are great moments — albeit few and far between.

Gladness and joy are very similar, sometimes practically indistinguishable. There are, however, three basic differences. (1) Gladness can be illusory whereas joy is always true; (2) Gladness is transitory whereas joy is permanent; (3) Gladness is still essentially a feeling whereas joy is a state of being.

St. Augustine makes a distinction between gladness (*gaudium*) and joy (*beatitudinis*). He defines joy as "gladness *in the truth*" and points out that gladness can be caused by evil things as well as by good things, while joy is always good (because it is true). One can feel glad in sin. The adulterous husband feels "gladness" when with his lover in a clandestine rendezvous. A bank robber feels "gladness" when pulling off yet another perfect caper that leaves the police baffled. This is because there is a good gladness (a gladness over good things) and a wicked gladness (over evil things).

Where there is sin there can be gladness, but not joy. Because sin is a lie — and joy is the truth.

3rd Degree: Peace

Peace is the third degree of happiness. It consists in the absence of conflict and division, of anything that could disturb or trouble us. Like a glassy-smooth lake on a still August evening, peace is tranquility, serenity, interior calm. Gone are fear, worry, pain, tears. Gone are the stress of our share in the daily rat race, the anxiety of making ends meet, and the distress of personal failure. Peace is when everything turns out all right in the end.

True peace is attainable only in Heaven, the definitive finish line of our temporal marathon. Only there will everything really be "all right." Only there will every tear be wiped away once and for all. Only there will all wounds be healed, divisions mended, and all apprehension put to rest.

Here on earth we catch glimpses of this peace — just enough to know that we desire it with all our heart and soul.

We could almost say peace and happiness are the same thing. In fact, in Sacred Scripture peace takes on the meaning not only of the *absence* of all evil, but also the *presence* of all good. Yet in modern usage, peace is more commonly associated with repose and freedom from strife. In this sense peace is a necessary condition for happiness — but not happiness itself. Happiness is a *positive* good, not the absence of something else.

Especially for youth, peace can be unsatisfying. Young people want action and adventure; they desire to dream, to plan, to discover — *to live.* And happiness is life. For this reason it is sometimes difficult to help adolescents appreciate the happiness of Heaven. Too often they fear the monotony and tedium that accompany certain traditional expressions of Heaven as a place of rest and contemplation, of celestial choirs chanting repetitive psalms, forever and ever and ever. . .

Taking this into account, we must take one step further to uncover the true nature of happiness: joy.

4th Degree: Joy

Boëthius describes happiness as "a good which once obtained leaves nothing more to be desired. It is the perfection of all good things and contains in itself all that is good." Later on he adds, "Happiness is a state made perfect by the presence of everything that is good." This is true and perfect happiness. This is what we're really after.

Joy is the presence and enjoyment of goodness, and is made perfect in Heaven where joy becomes "beatitude," the full enjoyment of Goodness Himself.

Here is where the childish concept of Heaven proves insufficient. Heaven isn't just the *absence* of problems and pain, but the *presence* of every good thing. Jesus doesn't speak of Heaven as sitting on clouds playing the harp all day. The images He uses are those of banquets, feasts and wedding celebrations — a bit more attractive than eons of harp rehearsal.

St. Paul gets downright tongue-tied when trying to describe Heaven and settles for telling us, "Eye has not seen, nor ear heard, nor has it even entered into the heart of man, what God has prepared for those who love Him" (1 Cor 2:9).

Happiness is — and isn't — having everything you want. We don't always want what will really make us happy. An alcoholic wants a glass of whiskey. A misanthrope wants to be left alone. A dictator wants control over every other person on the face of the earth. To be happy, we need not only possess what we want, we must also learn *to want what is good*.

It seems, then, that in order to be happy we first must learn to desire what is good and then obtain it.

It is not the same to know what we want and to know how to get it. Everyone has his dreams in life, yet relatively few attain them. A young boy who spots what he considers to be a particularly attractive orange and white gecko in the pet shop will have to come up with some pretty compelling arguments to convince Mom that the scaly little monster would make a favorable addition to the family. Knowing what we want is the first step, but then comes the matter of getting it.

You can't just decide to be happy from one moment to the next. Happiness isn't an activity. It's not something you do, like skateboarding or window-shopping. Nor is it a mere product of our willpower. Happiness is a state of being. It is more an effect than an undertaking, more a consequence than a project.

Treasure Hunting

Let's return to Christ's parable of the treasure buried in the field, which we commented on in the first chapter of this book:

> The Kingdom of God is like a treasure buried in a field which someone has found; he hides it again, goes off happy, sells everything he owns and buys that field (Mt 13:44).

Note well: *the treasure is not for sale.* The treasure comes with the field. Happiness works the same way. It isn't for sale. You can't choose to be happy—directly—but only indirectly, through the use of your freedom in the decisions of your daily life.

So what's the secret? What is the field where

In Pursuit of Happiness

the treasure is buried? There are many different answers given to this seemingly simple question. A typical response that the world offers are the three P's: pleasure, power and possessions. As much as we recognize their inadequacy, still they hold a fascination for us and keep pulling and tugging at our desires.

The Three P's

1. Pleasure

Pleasure is nice. We all like it. There's no getting around it and there's no sense trying to convince ourselves of the contrary. The big question isn't whether pleasure is enjoyable, but whether pleasure is *enough*. Can pleasure fill the human spirit?

Anyone who has really experienced pleasure will assure us that pleasure is insufficient. The French Renaissance humanist, Michel Montaigne, asserts in the third book of his *Essais*, "I, who boast of embracing the pleasures of life so assiduously and so particularly, find in them, when I look at them thus minutely, virtually nothing but wind. Pleasures are greatly longed for, but once we have them in hand we realize they are vain and fleeting."

The Bible offers similar testimony of the insufficiency of pleasure to meet the needs of the human spirit. Qoheleth reflects on the value of self-indulgence in this particularly illustrative text:

I thought to myself, "Very well, I will try pleasure and see what enjoyment has to offer." [. . .] I resolved to have my body cheered with wine. . . I resolved to embrace folly to see what made mankind happy, and what men do under heaven in the few days they have to live.

I did great things: built myself palaces, planted vineyards; made myself gardens and orchards, planting every kind of fruit tree in them. I had pools made for watering the plantations; bought men slaves, women slaves. . . ; herds and flocks I had, too, more than anyone in Jerusalem before me.

I amassed silver and gold, the treasures of kings and provinces; acquired singing men and singing women and delights of the flesh and many concubines. So I grew great, greater than anyone in Jerusalem before me. . . I denied my eyes nothing they desired, refusing my heart no pleasure. . .

I then reflected on all that my hands had achieved and on all the effort I had put into its achieving. What vanity it all is, and chasing of the wind! (Ec 2:1-11).

Psychologists speak of the "law of saturation" and "desensitization" with regard to people's enjoyment of pleasures. The more we abandon ourselves to pleasures, the less satisfaction we derive from them. Like narcotics, the dosage of pleasure must continually be increased in order to glean the same amount of gratification. Thus (even from an Epicurean standpoint) we must control pleasure to appreciate it. This being the case, happiness must be sought elsewhere.

2. Power

Most people deny that they seek power. It isn't a pleasant topic. Yet because of our wounded nature and tendency to pride, we all desire superiority: to be served and not to serve, to be treated specially, to have things *our* way. This is power.

Power, like pleasure, does not bring happiness. If we feed our hunger for power instead of holding it in check, we are nourishing what is low and vile in ourselves. Since the desire for power is a passion, if we do not dominate it, it will dominate us. And once we hand over our freedom in this way, we can kiss happiness good-bye.

Some of the most tragic lives of history have been the lives of men obsessed by power: Nero, Napoleon, Hitler, Mussolini, to name a few of the most famous. Julius Caesar himself said that he would rather reign supreme in a small village than be second man in the Roman Empire.

The quest for power is a cancer. It eats away at our interior, allowing no peace. This isn't only for dictators and potentates, but for all of us.

This drive for power, even when satisfied by the achievement of its end, leaves an immense void in the soul. Consider the testimony of Abderrahman II, Caliph of the Kingdom of Córdoba till the year 961, in his last will and testament:

> I have reigned more than fifty years, in victory or peace. Loved by my subjects, feared by my enemies and respected by my allies. Riches and honors, power and pleasures awaited my call to come to me immediately. There is no earthly blessing that has eluded me. In this situation I have carefully noted down the days of pure and genuine happiness I have enjoyed. *They number fourteen.* O man, do not place your hopes in this earth.

At best, power is temporary and uncertain. At its worst, it is obsessive, converting a man into his own worst enemy. At the height of his reign, Joseph Stalin became so suspicious and fanatical he exterminated even his closest friends and collaborators, convinced they were hatching plots to overthrow him. More often than not power brings anxiety, not happiness.

3. Possessions

The human heart desires to possess. When an attractive item catches our eye we want it for ourselves. Happiness is closely tied to possession. When we have everything we need, everything we want, everything our heart desires, we must certainly be happy. The question at hand is not possession, but rather *what* we possess.

What does it mean to possess something? It means that something is *mine*. I don't possess something merely because I'm holding it in my hand or have it in my pocket. When I go to a friend's house and pick up a videotape, it doesn't become mine because I am holding it. It is temporarily in my possession — but not mine forever.

Is there any "thing" we can possess forever? At the turn of the century there were landowners in Mexico whose properties were wrenched from their hands in the name of the Agrarian Land Reform. What was theirs one day was someone else's the next. In 1929 there were individuals who owned millions of dollars in stocks on the New York Exchange. From one day to the next the bottom fell out of the market and they were left with nothing. All our goods are unstable and passing, and one day we will release them.

The paradoxical reality is, material things are not "possessible." We possess not what is external to us but what is internal: our soul, our freedom, our virtues. In a certain way we possess our *past*, all our thoughts, words and actions — the good, the bad and the ugly. What we possess most of all is ourselves. Our decisions and choices are really ours.

It is far more important to *be* than to *have*. Many people have a thousand and one things, but aren't happy. Having things doesn't do it. This is why there are so many suicides, so many divorces, so many psychological problems among the rich. This very week while I've been writing this chapter the suicides of three prominent businessmen have hit the front page of the newspapers.

Why did Jesus say, "Happy are the poor in spirit"? Because *things* don't satisfy. If we adhere to the fallacy that happiness comes from having things, it's no wonder depression sets in when, having acquired a tidy fortune, we find we're still empty inside. This is what it means to "chase the wind."

How artfully Dickens describes in *Great Expectations* the profound dissatisfaction experienced once we have everything money can buy. He places these words in young Pip's mouth after the latter comes into his fortune:

> We spent as much money as we could, and got as little for it as people could make up their minds to give us. We were always more or less miserable, and most of our acquaintances were in the same condition. There was a gay fiction among us that we were constantly enjoying ourselves, and a skeleton truth that we never did.

The three P's, then, are three barren fields. We can dig as we will. We can bring in picks, jackhammers and heavy machinery. In these fields we will discover no treasure, no happiness. We might unearth an odd trinket, enough to keep our interest up — like the forty-niners who spent their lives mining for gold after finding a miniature nugget or two. But we'll never strike it rich.

Not only do the three P's not furnish happiness, they easily become an obstacle to its attainment. Jesus recognized this and offered us the unlikely alternative: the evangelical counsels of poverty, chastity and obedience. Poverty (not impoverishment but detachment from things) frees the soul from attachment to possessions. Chastity (not repression but the correct use of our sexuality) frees us from attachment to pleasure. Obedience (not slavery but willing submission to God and legitimate authority) frees us from attachment to power and pride. Only when one's head is cleared from the intoxicating voice of these three Sirens — pleasure, power and possessions — can one effectively pursue true happiness.

THREE FRUITFUL FIELDS

If happiness isn't buried in the conventional fields proposed by materialistic society, where can we find it? The answer to this question is not sensational enough to hit the front cover of Hollywood tabloids. It's not a quick fix, like a miracle drug or a spot-remover. But then again, the field isn't the discovery, the *treasure* is.

Love

Love is the gift of self. The odd thing about this sort of giving is that we don't lose what we give. When we give money we have less money. When we offer our time we have less time. When we dispense food or clothing we have less of these. But when we give ourselves we wind up with more (not less) self.

Among O. Henry's numerous excellent short stories, one of the best is *The Gift of the Magi*. It is a tale of a young married couple — James Dillingham Young and his wife Della — who are barely able to scrape by on the meager income James brings home. They reside in a tiny flat in the city and struggle to make ends meet, but they are happy. As winter is coming on each saves up to buy the other the most splendid Christmas present possible. James' one prized possession is a gold pocket watch handed down to him by his father. Della decides the best gift she can offer him is a chain for his watch. Since the price of the chain she has her eye on is well beyond her means, she decides to sell her long, dark, beautiful hair.

James has his own plans. After scouting all

over town he finally comes upon the perfect gift for his darling wife: a set of tortoise-shell combs for her hair. Since they come to a price he can't nearly afford, he decides — yes, you guessed it — he decides to sell his pocket watch to pay for the combs.

This is what love is about. Ridiculous. Illogical. Foolish. But what is life without love? What sort of meaning will you try to artificially tack on to life if you try to live without love? This is a reality that is tough to rationalize, a mystery that doesn't admit of facile explanations. We are made in God's image and likeness, and God is love. Without love we become freaks of nature, strangers and puzzles to ourselves. Christ said that there is more happiness in giving than in receiving, and so it is. In self-forgetfulness and donation we encounter happiness.

This leads us to an important corollary which comes as a jolt to the modern mentality: *suffering and happiness are not two opposite poles!* Advertisers would have us believe that the solution to unhappiness is the elimination of pain. "Take a pill." "Take a vacation." "Take a drink." If we're entrenched in this mentality, it will be hard to understand the logic of love. Love doesn't circumvent suffering. The mystery of love is a mystery of sacrifice, of dying to oneself, of pouring oneself out for the good of another. This is why our "couch therapy"/"feel-good" culture is incapable of happiness: because we are incapable of love. And we are incapable of love because we are incapable of forgetting ourselves.

Strangely enough, some of the happiest persons are persons who have suffered. Armor-plating our heart to make it invulnerable to pain is to mutilate our humanity. You and I are made to love, and we find our fulfillment and happiness in this most sublime human activity. As Corneille said, "In the happiness of others, I seek my happiness."

The greatest obstacle to love is egotism or self-seeking. None of us is an island. Those closed in on themselves can never be happy because "it is not good for man to be alone" (Gn 2:18).

Not without reason is solitary confinement considered the severest of punishments. Whether others put up the walls to keep us inside or we erect them to keep others out is of little consequence. Our smallness and impotence are never so evident as when we are *all alone*. And no one is so alone as the person who is full of himself.

Egotism is to make oneself — instead of truth — the standard and measure of all things. It is an exaggerated concern for self, and our own little world and problems. Egotism is the search for what is easiest and most pleasant, instead of what is true, noble, and good. Egotism is individualistic, viewing others as fundamentally opposed to self. The egotist sees his neighbor as a rival, like two hyenas eying each other warily as they circle around the same kill. Mine or yours. "Solidarity" doesn't fit into this scheme. Instead of treating the other as a *person*, the egotist uses him to attain his own advantage.

Happiness and charity (love) go hand in hand. Since egotism destroys charity, it also frustrates happiness. As Fr. Maciel reflects in a letter written in 1977:

> Charity opens, egotism closes. Charity sustains our ideal, egotism reduces it. Charity sharpens our conscience and tenses our will, egotism dulls the conscience and twists the will toward other purposes. Charity perfects, egotism constricts. Charity prompts, is dynamic and apostolic.

Learning to love is what life is really all about. Since we will always tend toward self-seeking, due to our wounded nature, we need to be on guard to keep our egotism in check. By mastering self, we are free to love.

Fidelity

The second field is *fidelity*. Fidelity — or faithfulness — is the fruit and culmination of love. It is the capacity to commit ourselves, to live according to our word regardless of changing or adverse circumstances. The faithful person rises above the shifting sands of mere fortune to live in the freedom of self-dominion. Fidelity needs no poetry, because a faithful soul is the most beautiful poem that can be contemplated here on earth. Words are superfluous. It is a virtue characterized by its works, and most often is expressed in a silent, unsung way. Fidelity is *true* heroism because it is perfection and constancy.

Happiness consists in the agreement between "I should" and "I want." We all have in life two deep experiences, the deepest that can be had: the experience of *duty* and the experience of *freedom*. If you do what you should, you are doing your duty, your "I should." But if you do it freely — because you want to and not because you are obliged — then you are doing your "I want." When your "I should" and your "I want" coincide, you are happy. "I should" without "I want" produces an experience of slavery; "I want" without "I should" produces emptiness.

There are many good works that flare up like a rocket but fizzle out just as quickly. It is easy to begin with enthusiasm but difficult to maintain that same spirit throughout. An isolated act of heroism may be likened to a sprint. The heroism of fidelity is a marathon.

The Western world has shifted from a culture of fidelity to a culture of infidelity. Earlier, all our heroes were precisely heroes of fidelity: squires faithful to their knights, knights faithful to their king, kings faithful to their people and to their principles.

We have the faithfulness of Penelope, wife of Odysseus, who hoped against hope for twenty years for the return of her husband from Troy. She bravely fought off the hordes of suitors that came daily to woo her away and win her hand. We have the fidelity of Cordelia, daughter of King Lear, who stands by her father's side despite constant incomprehension. Or there is the fidelity of Dickens' Joe Gargery, loyal friend to Pip in spite of the latter's ingratitude.

Likewise the most hateful villains of history are those who betrayed another's trust. We still shudder remembering the treachery of Brutus, onetime friend of Julius Caesar, Benedict Arnold, traitor to his country, and of course Judas Iscariot, who handed over his Lord for thirty pieces of silver.

Nowadays, however, infidelity is extolled as the path to freedom and spontaneity. In times past, infidelity was understood for what it is: *betrayal*. Nowadays we call it by pretty names that soften the harsh reality. We call it "spreading our wings," "innocent experimentation," "flights of fancy."

Who are today's heroes? They are James Bond — a likable character — who goes from woman to woman like a butterfly flits from flower to flower. Today's heroes are soap opera characters who plot and cheat and conspire against spouses, friends and business partners. They are music and cinema stars, whose personal lives are often a reflection of the tragedies that they sing of or act out in their films. But a life of unfaithfulness, flashy and alluring as it might seem, is the surest path to emptiness and disillusionment imaginable. Happiness rests with the faithful.

Husband and wife, doctor and patient, lawyer and client, business partners — all these are relationships of trust. A person who is faithful to himself and his principles, to God and to others is a whole person, a complete person. This wholeness is a necessary ingredient for happiness.

God

At the risk of stating the obvious, I propose that the third fruitful field is *God*. Perhaps it is not so obvious. There is much debate today about the possibility of a totally "secular" ethics, apart from any reference to a Supreme Being. Is happiness possible apart from God? Many desperately assert that it is. And I say "desperately" because they are scared to death that in order to be truly happy they will have to recognize God.

Since we are spiritual beings, we go beyond what is finite and limited to seek the Absolute. The human spirit looks to the infinite, never satisfied with any quantity of finite goods. After gorging ourselves on all the pleasures, adventures and possessions the world has to offer, our unsatisfied spirit looks further and inquires, "Is there nothing more?"

We seek and do not find because we seek right and left and around us and under us, but fail to seek above us. The only thing capable of filling us is God, because only God is infinite. The infinite cavity within us can only be filled by an infinite being. Blaise Pascal, in his *Pensées*, offers a similar diagnosis of our insatiable search for happiness: "The infinite abyss can only be filled by an infinite and immutable object, that is to say, only by God Himself."

Closer to our own day, C.S. Lewis, in his most popular work, *Mere Christianity*, explains why happiness without God is nothing but a pipe dream:

> What Satan put into the heads of our remote ancestors was the idea that they could [. . .] invent some sort of happiness for themselves outside God, apart from God. And out of that hopeless attempt has come nearly all that we call human history — money, poverty, ambition, war, prostitution, classes, empires, slavery — the long, terrible story of man trying to find something other than God which will make him happy.
>
> The reason why it can never succeed is this. God made us: invented us as a man

invents an engine. A car is made to run on petrol, and it would not run properly on anything else. Now God designed the human machine to run on Himself. He Himself is the fuel our spirits were designed to burn, or the food our spirits were designed to feed on. There is no other. That is why it is just no good asking God to make us happy in our own way without bothering about religion. God cannot give us a happiness and peace apart from Himself, because it is not there. There is no such thing.

Since the human person is one, all the dimensions of the life of that person are tied together. Happiness is not an isolated element independent from the other aspects of life. All values — happiness included — form a network and mutually support each other. Our many decisions, aided by the light and drive of conscience, are the branches that come together in the solid trunk of a mature personality, rooted in freedom. Happiness is the fruit of the tree. And where there are healthy roots, trunk and branches, there will always be fruit.

The key to finding things is to look where they are. Happiness is in God, so we shouldn't expect to find it elsewhere. The good things of this earth are but signposts that point to the Supreme Good. The trick is not to confuse the signposts with the point of arrival. As long as we realize that we are on a journey, we will have a traveler's joy. A traveler — a pilgrim — has the happiness of hope, the certainty of possessing in the future what he does not yet fully possess. One day not too far off, when the journey is done, we will know the happiness of arrival.

Values are not learned as facts are learned; they are assimilated. They are not taught, but passed on by testimony. If we are to bring happiness to the men and women of our times, it will not be through fine speeches or clever arguments, but only through the example of authentic lives grounded in real values. The only way to get beyond the shallow and subjective value-hopping of our times is to grasp hold of true values and hold them up so that their beauty and goodness may be appreciated.